Trevor Owen

THE BASIS AND ESSENTIALS
OF ITALIAN

THE BASIS AND ESSENTIALS SERIES

OF TEXT BOOKS ON MODERN LANGUAGES

GENERAL EDITOR: Charles Duff

Formerly Lecturer at the Institute of Education, University of London

THE BASIS AND ESSENTIALS OF FRENCH
by Charles Duff

THE BASIS AND ESSENTIALS OF GERMAN
by Charles Duff and Richard Freund

THE BASIS AND ESSENTIALS OF SPANISH
by Charles Duff

THE BASIS AND ESSENTIALS OF ITALIAN
by Charles Duff

THE BASIS AND ESSENTIALS OF WELSH
by J. P. Vinay, M.A. and W. O. Thomas, B.A.
ALL PRICE 5/-

THE BASIS AND ESSENTIALS OF RUSSIAN
by Charles Duff and Anissime Krougliakoff
(PRICE 6/-)

THE BASIS AND ESSENTIALS OF PORTUGUESE
AND READER (in one volume) by Charles
Duff (PRICE 7/6)

*READING AND PRACTICE BOOKS
TO ACCOMPANY THE ABOVE*

FRENCH, GERMAN, SPANISH, AND ITALIAN
(PRICE 4/6)
RUSSIAN (PRICE 5/-)

These brilliant handbooks are now published by Nelsons for the Orthological Institute, London. Their author describes them as " a first approximation " to Basic French, German, Spanish, etc. Like the " Basic English " sponsored by the Institute, they are built up on scientific principles, and in their clear-cut and straightforward approach, no less than in their reduction of vocabulary to its essentials, they have an obvious affinity with the Basic method.

The books are printed in the famous Gill Sans-Serif type, which makes memorizing much easier by its unequalled " attention value."

" THE MORNING POST "

THE
BASIS AND ESSENTIALS
OF ITALIAN

Containing all that
must be known of Grammar
and Vocabulary in order to
express the most frequently
recurring ideas

Being a first approximation to a " BASIC ITALIAN "

by

CHARLES DUFF

" Chi ben incomincia è a metà dell'opera "

Third Edition, revised

Published for
The Orthological Institute
London

by

THOMAS NELSON & SONS, LTD.
3, Henrietta Street, Covent Garden, London, W.C.2.
Edinburgh, Paris, Toronto, New York

First Published January, 1938
Second (revised) Edition 1943
Reprinted March, 1944
Reprinted September, 1944
Reprinted August, 1945
Reprinted June, 1946
Third (revised) Edition, June, 1950
Reprinted September, 1951

Printed in Great Britain by
R. I. SEVERS, LTD., CAMBRIDGE

INTRODUCTION

The books in this series present a method of approach to the study of foreign languages based upon a simple principle : *That the part of any language to be studied and mastered FIRST, is the part required to cover the essentials of ordinary communication and to express the most frequently recurring ideas.* It is hoped that, as a result of further experience, it may be possible from the material assembled to produce for each language a BASIC SYSTEM, on similar lines to Mr. C. K. Ogden's Basic English, of which the superb economy is demonstrated by the fact that in it 850 words do the work of over 20,000.

The student who uses this little book for the study of Italian may be assured that what he or she is learning is the *minimum of essential material* which must be known; that he or she is not wasting time learning a mass of useless and complex grammar; and that the Vocabulary in Part II of the book, together with the Grammar in Part I, will enable him or her to make sense of an average page of Italian, and to express nine out of ten of the ideas of everyday life.

The first goal of the student must be to get *as rapidly as possible to the READING STAGE.* Hence, for a start, it is unnecessary to master every line and page of grammar on a first approach. For a beginning, it is better to concentrate upon general principles and above all on the memorizing of words. VOCABULARY IS THE MOST IMPORTANT PART OF LANGUAGE: and whatever the purpose may be for which Italian is studied, the vocabulary in this book will be found to be of vital importance. When the reading stage is reached, a new vista appears : the student finds that the language is a living instrument, a means of receiving *ideas* and transmitting them, and not a mere collection of words and grammatical forms. From that moment interest increases and progress becomes more rapid, and by persistent revision of the grammar and vocabulary, by constant reading, and by hearing Italian spoken, ability to speak it soon follows. With this book it is possible to attain the reading stage with a minimum of effort and no waste of time. For practice in reading, the student should follow it up with the *Italian Basis and Essentials Reader* in the present series of books from the same publishers.

I wish to acknowledge my indebtedness to *La Grammática degl'Italiani* by Trabalza and Allodoli (3rd Edition, Florence, 1934—XII). It is probably the best modern statement of Italian grammar, and it is the book which I would recommend to the student who wishes to pursue his studies. Also, I wish to thank my friends Fr. Giovanni Cotta, Mr. E. Ernest Lentz, Dr. Hermann Walde, and Fr. Angelo Romano, for their great kindness in the laborious task of proof-reading, and for many valuable suggestions (they are all experienced teachers) which I have incorporated.

I shall always be grateful to receive suggestions, which should be addressed to me c/o The Orthological Institute, 10 King's Parade, Cambridge, England.

London, September 1937.   CHARLES DUFF.

Suggestions from correspondents, especially in the American and British forces and services in Italy, are responsible for a number of further improvements. They are the result of practical use of the book for the practical purposes of life, in which it has stood up to almost every sort of test and come out extremely well. My thanks are due to those correspondents and to Mr. Raimundo Bernardi for the help he gave me with the previous edition.

London, May 1945.   C. D.

CONTENTS

Part II
THE ESSENTIAL VOCABULARY

Part 1
THE BASIS OF GRAMMAR

ALPHABET AND PRONUNCIATION

The alphabet is the same as in English, except that **K, X, Y** and **W** are never used in Italian, and **J** very rarely (in some old proper names). **X** is found only in the word **Ex** in such expressions as **EX-MINISTRO**, *Ex-minister*, etc.

There are two accents: the grave (ˋ) and the acute (ˊ), of which the grave is the more important.

The grave accent (ˋ) has two uses: (1) It is placed over a terminal vowel to indicate that it must be stressed—for example, **lunedì** (*Monday*) is pronounced *loonaydee'*, and **onestà** (*honesty*) is pronounced *onnestah'*, in each case the last syllable being more strongly stressed than the others. That is the general use of the grave accent. But it is also used (2) to differentiate words of one syllable which would otherwise be identically written: thus, **è** with the accent means *is*, and **e** means *and*. Similarly: **chè** means *because*, and **che** means *that*; **dì** means *day*, and **di** means *of*; **là, lì**, mean *there* and **la, li** mean *the*; **sì** means *yes*, and **si** means *one's self*; **nè** means *nor*, and **ne** means *some, of it, of them;* **dà** means *gives*, and **da** means *by* or *from*.

The acute accent tends to fall into disuse,[1] except in text books and dictionaries, but it is a useful guide for the foreigner. In words of more than two syllables, it is used to indicate stress when this does not follow the general rule (for which see below). Thus: **único,** (*single, only*) is pronounced *oo'nico;* **pópolo,** (people) is pronounced *po'pŏoloh.*

---

[1] Strictly, there is *no* acute accent in Italian written by Italians for Italians. It is used throughout this book as a *sign to indicate stress*, which when very irregular is also indicated by printing the stressed vowel conspicuously : **Le fOrbici,** *the scissors.*

¶ *GENERAL RULE FOR ACCENTUATION OR STRESS.*

THE STRESSED SYLLABLE OF EVERY ITALIAN WORD IS THE LAST BUT ONE UNLESS INDICATED BY A GRAVE OR ACUTE ACCENT.

Thus: **caro** (*dear*) is pronounced *cah'roh;* **delicato** (*delicate*) is pronounced *delicah'toh;* **virtù** (*virtue*) is pronounced *veertoo';* **ridícolo** (*ridiculous*) is pronounced *reedeé'cŏhloh.*

In the above simple rule the student finds a complete solution of what is in some other languages (English and Russian, for example) the difficult problem of stress, and this, with the other Italian custom of giving *one fixed value to each vowel and consonant,* takes from Italian pronunciation those major terrors so common in other languages.

¶ *PURITY OF ITALIAN VOWEL SOUNDS.*

Yet, there is one difficulty which the English-speaking learner must overcome at the outset. He must avoid the English tendency to utter ' impure ' vowel sounds. Take, for example, the English word *No* as spoken by a ' cultured ' person. It is not a pure *oh* sound. It has a very slight *oo* or *i* sound tacked on to it. This addition of a slight auxiliary vowel-sound to most vowels is a characteristic of the English language, and makes ' cultured ' English pronunciation so difficult for the foreigner. It should be noted that Irish, Scotch and Welsh and some other English-speaking peoples do not always pronounce their vowels in this manner, and for them Italian pronunciation comes easier.

ALL ITALIAN VOWEL SOUNDS ARE PURE. This is of very great importance, and the student must from the outset make every possible effort to pronounce his vowels with the utmost clarity and purity. Thus, when saying the Italian word **no**, let the *oh* be round, clear and *finish with a pure oh sound.* Let the beginner not hesitate to give full value to the simple vowel sounds noted below, repeating them again and again until he has eliminated every tendency to treat them as impure English vowels.

¶ *THE SIMPLE VOWELS.*

A, pronounce as *ah*, almost as the **a** in *father, art, arm.*
E   ,,   ,, *eh,*   ,,   ,,   ,, **ê** in *fête,* or *a* in *lame.*
I   ,,   ,, *ee*   ,,   ,,   ,, **ee** in *bee* or *e* in *me.*
O   ,,   ,, *oh*   ,,   ,,   ,, **oh** in *note* or *not.*
U   ,,   ,, *oo*   .,   ..   ., **oo** in *cool, fool,* or *u* in *rule,* and the same sound shorter as in *to.*

¶ *DIPHTHONGS.*

When two or more vowels come together in Italian, each is pronounced clearly. When **i** and **u** come before other vowels the **i** and **u** are pronounced very short. Thus: **paura** (*fear*) is pronounced *pahŏŏ'ra;* **Europa** (*Europe*) is pronounced *Ehŏŏroh'pah,* but **bianco** (*white*) is pronounced almost *byahn'co;* and **buono** (*good*) is pronounced almost *bwoh'no.*

The **i** and **u** coming before other vowels make the only true diphthongs in Italian. All other vowel combinations should be pronounced to give a clear cut value to each vowel. Thus: **miei** (*mine*, masc. pl.) is pronounced *mieh'ee.* Endings in **-io, -ia** make usually one syllable pronounced *yo* or *ya.*

3

¶ *ELISION OF VOWELS FOR EUPHONY.*

When a word ends with an unaccented vowel, and the next word begins with a vowel, then the vowel at the end of the first word is dropped. Thus: **tutto** (*all, altogether*) and **altro** (*other, otherwise*) when written together become **tutt'altro** (*quite otherwise*). This is for euphony and, as will be seen later,[1] is very frequent in Italian

¶ *CONSONANTS.*

Italian consonants are pronounced like the English, with the following exceptions : **C, G, H, R, S, Z.**

NOTE WELL :

  C, before **e** or **i** is pronounced like the English *ch* in *Church* or *cheap*. Thus **cena** (*supper*) pronounce *chay'na*. **Città** (*city*) pronounce *chittah'*—sound each **t** distinctly and put the stress on the last syllable. The word **cello** in English is borrowed from Italian, and so the **c** is pronounced like our *ch*. **C** before **a, o, u** or a consonant is always pronounced like the English *k*. Thus: **banco** (*bank*), pr. *bahn'ko*.

  CC, before **e** or **i** is pronounced like double English *ch*. Thus: **accento** (*accent*), pr. *ahtchen'toh*.

  CH, is always pronounced like English *ch* in *chemist* or *k*. Thus: **chiesa** (*church*), pr. *keeay'sah*. **perchè** (*why, because*), pr. *perkay*.

  G, before **e** or **i** sounds like English *g* in *gem* or *j* in *jest*. Thus: **gelo** (*frost*), pr. *jay'loh*.

[1] See, for example, page 10, the contractions, etc.

4

Giorno (*day*), pr. *jiohr'no*. **g**, before **a, o, u** and a consonant is like the English hard *g* in *get, gone*. Thus: **gallo** (*cock*), pr. *gal'lo*.

GG, followed by **e** or **i** is pronounced like English *d-j*. Thus: **oggi** (*to-day*), pr. *odj'ee*.

GH, is always pronounced hard like *g* in *get* or *gh* in *ghetto*. Thus: **ghirlanda** (*garland, wreath*), pr. *geerlan'da*.

GL, when followed by the vowel **i** is said to be ' liquid ' (like French *ll mouillé*, or Spanish *ll*) and has a sound like the English *-lli-* in *brilliant* or *million*. Thus: **bottiglia** (*bottle*), pr. *botteell'ya*. **Egli, gli,** (*he, to him*), pr. *ayl'yee, lyee*. But note that Italian **gl** is pronounced as in English when followed by an **i** that is followed by another consonant. Thus: **negligente** (*negligent*) pr. *naygleejen'tay*. **Anglicano** (*anglican*), pr. *anglicah'no*.

GN, is also called a ' liquid ' sound. It resembles the French *gn*—in *Boulogne*, or the Spanish *ñ* in *Señor* and the English *-ni-* in *union* or *onion*. Thus: **bagno** (*bath*), pr. *bahn'yo*. **Incógnito** (*incognito*), pr. *eencon'yeeto*.

GU, is always pronounced like the English *gw*. Thus: **guerra** (*war*), pr. *gwerra;* **guida** (*guide*), pr. *gwee'da*.

H, is always silent in Italian. Thus: **ho, hai, ha** (*I have, thou hast, he has*), pr. *oh, ah'ee, ah*.

QU, is always pronounced like English *kw*. Thus: **questo** (*this*) pr. *kwes'to*.

R, is well rolled and pronounced with the tip of the tongue against the teeth. Thus: **raro** (*rare*), pr. *rah'ro*.

5

S, is hard, like English *ss* in *moss*: **casa** (*house*) pr. *kassa*. Followed by a consonant, it is like English *s* in *some, such*. Thus: **spedire** (*to expedite, despatch*), pr. *sspaydeer'ay*. **sarto** (*tailor*), pr. *ssahr'to*.

Note that initial **s** followed by a consonant is called ' impure s ' and it is pronounced soft like English *s* in *rose* when it comes before : b, d, g, l, m, n, r or v.[1] Thus: **svelto** (*quick, nimble*) pr. *zvel'to*.

SC, before **e** and **i** is pronounced like English *sh* in *ship*. Thus **scena** (*scene*), pr. *shay'na*. **scelta** (*choice*), pr. *shel'ta*. Before **-a, -o, -u,** it is pronounced like *sk*, **scusa**.

SCH, is always pronounced like *sch* in *school* or *sk* in *skip*. Thus **schiavo** (*slave*), pr. *skeeah'vo*, almost *skyah'vo*.

Z, if not at the beginning of a word, is pronounced like *ts* in *bits*. Thus: **scienza** (*science*), pr. *sheeaynt'sa*. If at the beginning of a word, it often sounds like *dz* in *adze*: **zelo** (*zeal*), pr. *dzay'lo*, **zero** (*zero*) pr. *dzay'ro*. Learn these two essential words.

ZZ, is generally pronounced like *ts* in *bits*, **Bellezza** (*beauty*), pr. *bellayt'sa*. Note, however, that it is pronounced like *dz* in the following: **mezzo** (*half, middle*), pr. *med'dzo*; **dozzina** (*dozen*) pr. *doddzeen'a*. Also in verbs ending **-zzare**. Thus: **scandalizzare** (*scandalise*) pr. *scandahleedzah'rey*. **Analizzare,** analyse ; **fertilizzare,** to *fertilise*. Learn these words, especially **mezzo** and **dozzina,** as they are essential.

[1] The English phrase " Roving blackguard " contains all these consonants except **M.**

¶ DOUBLE CONSONANTS.

Italian consonants have fixed values, and each consonantal sound is pronounced clearly. The English student is apt to pronounce indistinctly, a tendency which must be avoided. Remember especially to pronounce a double consonant *twice*. Thus: **Agnello** (*lamb*), pr. *ahnyel'lo*. **Fratello** (*brother*), pr. *frahtel'lo*. **Braccio** (*arm*), pr. *braht'cho*. **Fiamma** (*flame*), pr. *fyahm'ma*.

¶ WARNING :

The student must realise clearly that all ' imitated ' pronunciation and English equivalents such as those given above are makeshifts. Strictly, every Italian letter and combination of letters should be regarded as representing a sound or sounds quite different from anything in English. These makeshift equivalents are a rough and ready guide to Italian pronunciation, but they can never adequately take the place of a native teacher. At any cost, the serious student should try to find a native to teach him the elements of pronunciation— it will repay him tenfold, and probably avoid the acquisition at the outset of a faulty Italian accent. A faulty accent so acquired tends to remain; it is *extremely* difficult to eliminate afterwards. If no native teacher is available, listen to gramophone records of speech or singing, of which many are available. Or listen to broadcasts from Italian stations. Never be afraid to speak to Italians—they are a loquacious race and will be only too delighted to help. Roll your **r**'s, pronounce your vowels ' pure ' and give each consonant and especially double consonants, full value. Italian pronunciation is easy, but it needs careful attention in the beginning stage; its keynote is

7

clarity and distinctness. Its characteristic when well pronounced is softness and a mellifluous beauty of sound. In this respect, it has probably no equal amongst European languages; and therefore the pronunciation is worthy of close attention.

ARTICLES

The words *the* and *a* are called articles, the former the definite, the latter the indefinite article.

¶ *DEFINITE ARTICLE.*

For *the*, the Italian equivalents are:

il, before a masculine noun
lo, before a masculine noun beginning ⎫ in the
    with an **s** impure or **z** ⎬ singular.
la, before a feminine noun ⎭
i, before a masculine noun
gli, before a masculine noun, beginning ⎫ in the
    with a vowel, **s** impure or **z** ⎬ plural.
le, before a feminine noun ⎭

Examples:

Singular	Plural
il padre, *the father.*	**i padri,** *the fathers.*
lo stato, *the state.*	**gli stati,** *the states.*
la città, *the city.*	**le città,** *the cities.*

NOTE:

lo is shortened to **l'** before words beginning with a vowel.

gli may be shortened to **gl'** before words beginning with **i**.

8

la is shortened to **l'** before words beginning with a vowel.

le is shortened to **l'** only before words beginning with an **e**.

Examples:

Masculine	**l'amico** *the friend* **l'italiano** *the Italian*	**gli amici** *the friends* **gl'italiani** *the Italians*
Feminine	**l'ambizione** *the ambition* **l'erba** *the grass*	**le ambizioni** *the ambitions* **l'erbe** *the grasses*

¶ DEFINITE ARTICLE CONTRACTED WITH PRE-POSITIONS.

When the definite article occurs with certain prepositions, the article and preposition are combined to form a contraction. Thus, instead of writing **a** (*to*) **il** (*the*), one writes **al**.

And instead of **da il,** (*from, or by the*) one says and writes **dal**, etc.

Contraction is of frequent occurrence in Italian —it is used in the interest of euphony—and the student must become familiar with it at an early stage. Hence, although the following table is given here for reference, and need not necessarily be mastered thoroughly now, the sooner it is memorised the better.

The prepositions which form contractions with the article are:

A, *to, at;* **CON**, *with;* **DA**, *by, from;* **DI**, *of;* **IN**, *in;* **PER**, *for, by;* **SU**, *on.*

	il,	lo,	l'	la	i	gli	le
A	al	allo	all'	alla	ai	agli	alle
CON	col	(collo)	coll'	colla	coi	(cogli)	(colle)
DA	dal	dallo	dall'	dalla	dai	dagli	dalle
DI	del	dello	dell'	della	dei	degli	delle
IN	nel	nello	nell'	nella	nei	negli	nelle
PER	pel	(pello)	pell'	(pella)	(pei)	(pegli)	(pelle)
SU	sul	sullo	sull'	sulla	sui	sugli	sulle

NOTE. **dei** and **ai** are further contracted to **de'** and **a'** before an **i** : **sullo** and **sui** are not very frequent ; and **con lo** and **con la** are more common than **collo, colla**, etc.; also **per lo** and **per la** are more common than **pello** and **pella**, etc.[1] **Pelle** is quite rare.

¶ TRANSLATION OF " SOME " OR " ANY."

The preposition **DI** combined with the definite article expresses *some* or *any*. Thus :

> **DEL VINO** means *some wine*.
>
> **DEI LIBRI** means *some books*.

Voglio bere di questa birra, *I wish to drink some of this beer.*

¶ USAGE WHICH DIFFERS FROM ENGLISH.

The article is used in Italian :

(a) For the hour : **Che ora è?** *What o'clock is it? It is one o'clock.* **È l'una.** *Two o'clock:* **le due.** (The words **ora, ore,** meaning *hour-s,* are understood after **una** and **due**). *It is a quarter past eleven:* **Sono le undici ed[2] un quarto** (Literally : *They are the eleven (hours) and a quarter.* See page 23).

(b) For the date: **Quanti ne abbiamo del mese?** *What day of the month is it?* **Ne abbiamo dieci.** *It is the tenth.* **Il 25 di Gennaio, del 1938.** (On) *the 25th January, 1938.* (See page 22).

[1] In the pages which follow, the less important material will be found in small type.
[2] **Ed** is used for **e** (*and*) before a vowel.

10

(c) Before titles and Signore, Signora, Signorina. *Duke Peter:* **Il duca Pietro.** *Mr. X has arrived from London:* **Il signor X è arrivato da Londra.** *Mrs. Jones is here:* **La signora Jones è qui.**

(d) Before names of countries. **L'Italia,** *Italy.* **L'Inghilterra,** *England.* **La Francia,** *France.*
  (NOTE. **In Francia,** *in France,* but **Nella Gran Bretagna,** *in Great Britain*).

(e) The article is repeated before several nouns in Italian. Thus: **ho comprato l'inchiostro, la carta ed il libro,** *I have bought the ink, paper and the book.*

(f) To express 'a' in such phrases as *Five francs a pound, Three times a week;* **Cinque franchi la libbra; tre volte la settimana.**

(g) When a noun is used in a general sense or to the fullest extent of its meaning: **L'uomo è mortale,** *Man is mortal.* **i cavalli sono útili,** *Horses are useful.*

(h) To express the possessive case the article is combined with the preposition **DI** *(of).* Thus, *The mother's secret* becomes *The secret of the mother:* **Il segreto della madre.**

¶ *THE INDEFINITE ARTICLE.*

UN before a masculine noun.
UNO before S impure or Z.
UNA before a feminine noun.
UN' before a feminine noun beginning with a vowel.
—all equivalent to the English *a* or *an.*

Examples:

> **UN LAGO,** *a lake.*
> **UNO ZÍO,** *an uncle.*
> **UNA FIGLIA,** *a daughter.*
> **UN'ORA,** *an hour.*

Generally the indefinite article is used in Italian as in English, but note the following:—

OMIT THE ARTICLE: (a) When stating a nationality, rank, profession or trade:

11

sono tedesco: *am a German.*
sono capitano: *I am a captain.*
È artista: *He is an artist.*
È sarto: *He is a tailor.*

(b) before a noun in apposition:

Vittorio Emanuele, re d'Italia: *Vittorio Emanuele,* (the) *King of Italy.*

NOTE: **a casa,** *at home;* **a scuola,** *at school;* **in camera,** *in the room;* **di cucina,** *of the kitchen;* **con amore,** *lovingly.* **Gli** (and never **i**) is used before the plural word "Gods." Thus: **Gli dei**—*the gods.*

NOUNS

" A noun is a word used for naming some *person* or *thing.*"

¶ GENDER.

There are two genders for Italian nouns : masculine and feminine.

RULES.—(1) The names of men and male animals are másculine; the names of women and female animals are feminine.

(2) Nouns ending in **-o** or a consonant are masculine, and nouns ending in **-a, -ione** or **-ù** are feminine. Examples:

il padre, *the father.*   **la madre,** *the mother.*
il giuoco, *the game.*   **la casa,** *the house.*
la colazione, *the meal.*   **la virtù,** *virtue.*

Note the following: **La mano** (plur. **le mani**) *the hand ;* **muro** (masc.) *wall,* plur. **i muri** means *walls of a room* and plural **le mura** (fem.) means *external walls.* **Paio** (masc.) *pair,* plur., **paia** (fem.); **riso** (masc.) *laugh,* plur., **risa** (fem.); **centinaio** (masc.) *hundred,* plur. **centinaia** (fem.); **migliaio,** (masc.) *a thousand,* plur. **migliaia ; uovo** (masc.) *egg,* plur. **uova** (fem.)[1]; **miglio** (masc.) *mile,* plur. **miglia** (fem.)

Apart from the above simple rules, which cover the majority of Italian nouns, the student is advised to

[1] **ovo, ova** in poetry.

12

learn the gender of each noun as it is met—this is the safest rule of all, and will enable him to master the many exceptions.

On a *second* perusal of this book (no need to learn them now) the following more elaborate rules will be found useful:—

Rules:		Exceptions:
Nouns ending in	**are of the masculine gender**	
-o		**Mano,** *hand;* **eco,** *echo;* and some poetical words. Nouns ending in **-E,** some are masculine and some are feminine, as **padre,** *father;* **madre,** *mother.* It is difficult to give safe rules for nouns ending in **-e;** yet the terminations **-me, -nte -one, -pe** and **-re,** are masculines except:
-e		
-me		**Arme,** *weapon;* **fame,** *hunger;* **corrente,** *stream;* **fonte,** *fountain;* **fronte,** *front;* **gente,** *people;* **mente,** *mind.*
-nte		
-one		**Canzone,** *song.* See **-ione.**
-pe		**Ape,** *bee;* **volpe,** *fox;* **siepe,** *hedge;* **rupe,** *rock;* **stirpe,** *race.*
-re		**cárcere,** *prison;* **cénere,** *ashes;* **febbre,** *fever;* **lepre,** *hare;* **scure,** *axe;* **tigre,** *tiger;* **torre,** *tower.*
Nours ending in	**are of the feminine gender**	
-a		Names of men, titles and professions, as: **Andrea; papa,** *pope;* **duca,** *duke;* **poeta, oculista,** etc. But feminine are: **santità,** *holiness;* **maestà,** *majesty;* **altezza,** *highness;* **eccellenza,** *excellency* and **guida,** *a guide;* **guardia,** *a guard;* and **sentinella,** *a sentinel.*
		Nouns derived from Greek as: **anatema,** *anathema;* **clima,** *climate;* **diadema, diploma, pianeta,** *planet;* **poema, panorama,** etc. etc.
-ione		**Milione,** *million;* **muraglione,** *wall;* **piccione,** *pigeon;* **settentrione,** *north.*
-i		**Abbicci,** *a, b, c;* **barbagianni,** *owl;* **brindisi,** *a toast;* **stuzzicadenti,** *toothpick;* **cavastivali,** *bootjack;* **Parigi,** *Paris;* **Tamigi,** *Thames;* **dì,** *day;* and the days of the week except **Doménica.**
-u		**Corfù** and **Perù.**

13

¶ *TO FORM THE FEMININE OF MANY NOUNS.*

Many masculine nouns may be made feminine by changing the ending **-O** into **-A.** Thus:

Ragazzo, *boy,* **ragazza,** *girl;* **cuoco,** *cook* (m.), **cuoca,** *cook* (fem.); **cittadino,** *citizen* (m.) **cittadina,** *citizen* (fem.).

This is a most useful rule—one which doubles a whole section of one's vocabulary.

¶ *PLURAL OF NOUNS.*

There are five simple rules for the formation of the plural of Italian nouns:

I. Nouns ending in a vowel, excepting feminine nouns ending in **-A,** change the final vowel into **-i:**—

il poeta, *the poet.*	**i poeti,** *poets.*
la madre, *the mother.*	**le madri,** *mothers.*
il padre, *the father.*	**i padri,** *fathers.*

II. Feminine nouns ending in **-A** change this to **-e:**—

la ragazza, *the girl*	**le ragazze,** *girls.*
la porta, *door.*	**le porte,** *doors.*
l'ora, *hour.*	**le ore,** *hours.*

III. Nouns ending in **-io,** omit the **-o** in the plural:—

Il figlio, *the son.*	**i figli,** *the sons.*

But if the **i** is accented as **lo zío,** *the uncle,* then the **-o** is changed to **-i.** Thus: **gli zíi,** *the uncles.*[1]

---

[1] The endings **-io, -ia** usually make one syllable: the **i** is rarely accented. This helps to explain why **fíglio** has the stress on the **i,** and why the plural is **figli** and not **fíglii.**

NOTE.—Nouns ending in **-ca, -ga, -co, -go**, besides changing the **a** and **o**, add **h** after the **c** or **g** to preserve euphony :

il duca, the duke.	**i duchi,** dukes.
il collega, the colleague.	**i colleghi,** colleagues.
il fico, the fig.	**i fichi,** figs.
il lago, the lake.	**i laghi,** lakes.

NOTE ALSO.—

il porco, pig.	**i porci,** pigs.
l'amico, friend.	**gli amici,** friends.

and

il Greco, the Greek.	**i Greci,** Greeks.
médico, doctor	**médici,** doctors.
crítico, critic.	**crítici,** critics.

IV. Most nouns ending in **-cia** or **-gia** omit the **i** in the plural:—

La pioggia, rain.	**Le piogge,** rains.
La provincia, province.	**Le province,** provinces.

V. Words ending in a consonant or stressed vowel do not change in the plural :

il re, the king.	**i re,** the kings.
la difficoltà, the difficulty.	**le difficoltà,** the difficulties.

¶ *IRREGULAR PLURALS.*

Singular	Plural
ALA (f), wing.	**ALI,** wings.
BUE, ox.	**BUOI,** oxen.
DIO, God.	**DEI,** gods.
MILLE, thousand.	**MILA,** thousands.
UOMO, man.	**UOMINI,** men.[1]

AND NOTE.—**Le fórbici,** scissors (no singular).

[1] compare Latin **homo, homines.**

15

ADJECTIVES

" An adjective is a word used to describe the quality of a noun."

RULE.—In Italian the adjective agrees in gender and number with the noun, and usually follows it. This rule applies wherever there is one or more adjectives qualifying the noun.[1]

Most adjectives end in **-o** in the masculine and **-a** in the feminine, but those ending in **-e** do not change in the feminine. Thus:—

nuovo, *new* (masc.).

nuova, *new* (fem.).

diligente, *diligent* (masc. and fem.).

The plural of adjectives is formed according to the same rules as the plural of nouns (See page 14). Thus:—

nuovo, nuovi; *new*, masc. sing. and plur.

nuova, nuove; *new*, fem. sing. and plur.

diligente, diligenti ; *diligent*, (masc., fem., sing. or plur.).

Euphonic changes:—

bianco, *white* (masc.) plur.: **bianchi** (masc.) **bianche** (fem.).

lungo, *long* (masc.) plur. **lunghi, lunghe** (fem.).

tedesco, *German*, (masc.) plur.: **tedeschi, tedesche.**

Adjectives ending in **-io** drop the **o** in the plural: **savio,** *wise*, pl. **savi.** (fem. plur. **savie**).

[1] The student who knows French will appreciate as he advances in Italian that the position of adjectives is often determined by taste, but for the present he should keep to the rule given above.

16

¶ *ADJECTIVES WHICH PRECEDE THE NOUN.*

The following seven adjectives are placed before their nouns:—

bello, *beautiful* **brutto,** *ugly*
buono, *good* **cattivo,** *bad*
grande, *big, great* **píccolo,** *small*
santo, *saint*

Bello, buono, grande and **santo** are usually abbreviated (but never before **z** or **s** impure) in the masculine singular, as follows:—

bel, buon, gran, san, before a consonant
bell', buon', grand,' sant' before a vowel.

The plural of **bel** is **bei.**

„ „ „ **bello**⎫ is **belli**—(**begli** before a vowel or
„ „ „ **bell'** ⎭ **s** impure, **begl'** before **i**).

¶ *COMPARISON.*

Superiority: (1) (2) (3)
  più (adjective) di or che
  più bello di
  more *beautiful* *than*
Inferiority: meno (adjective) di or che
  meno bello di
  less *beautiful* *than.*

THAN is translated by either **di** or **che**:—
  (a) by **di** before a noun, pronoun or number.
  (b) by **che** before an adjective, verb or adverb.

THUS: **Lo zio è più ricco del fratello,** *The uncle is richer than the brother.* **Egli ha più di tre sorelle,** *He has more than three sisters.* But : **Méglio tardi che mai,** *Better late than never.*

17

Equality :	(1)	(2)	(3)
	così	(adjective)	come
	così	bello	come
	as	*beautiful*	*as*

¶ *THE SUPERLATIVE.*

The Superlative is formed by placing the article before the comparative. Thus:—

il più ricco, *the richest* (masc.).
la più cattiva, *the worst* (fem.).
il meno brutto, *the least ugly* (masc.).
la meno bella, *the least beautiful* (fem.).

The word **molto** (*much, very*) is frequently used to form a sort of superlative: **È molto ricco,** *he is very* (i.e. superlatively) *rich.*

Another common superlative (in speech though not in writing) is formed by repeating the adjective.
L'inglese è difficile, difficile, *English is difficult, most difficult.* **Pian piano,** *very softly.*

And there is the Superlative Absolute, formed by dropping the last vowel of an adjective and adding **-ÍSSIMO.**

bravo, *brave.*	**bravíssimo,** *most brave.*
ricco, *rich.*	**ricchíssimo,** *most rich.*

Note the change in spelling **ricchíssimo,** for euphony.

Also in the comparative and superlative, the adjective usually follows the noun :

La città più bella, *The most beautiful city.*

I metalli utilíssimi agli uómini, *The most useful metals for men.*

18

¶ *IRREGULAR COMPARATIVES AND SUPERLATIVES.*

Positive.	Comp.	Sup.
alto,	**superiore,**	**supremo,**
high.	higher.	highest
buono,	**migliore,**	**il migliore,**
good.	better.	best.
cattivo,	**peggiore,**	**il peggiore,**
bad.	worse.	worst.
grande,	**maggiore,**	**il maggiore,**
big.	bigger.	biggest.
píccolo,	**minore,**	**il minore,**
small.	smaller.	smallest.

The above have also regular forms; **più alto,
il più alto,** etc.

Also note the following forms:
      sommo-a, *highest ;* **óttimo-a,** *the best ;* **péssimo-a,**
      the worst ; **mássimo,** *the greatest ;* **mínimo,** *the*
      smallest ; **acre,** *sharp,* **acérrimo,** *sharpest ;* **célebre,**
      celebrated, **celebérrimo,** *most celebrated ;* **integro,**
      unblemished, **integérrimo,** *most unblemished ;* **mísero,**
      wretched, **misérrimo,** *most wretched ;* **salúbre,** *healthy,*
      salubérrimo, *most healthy.*

¶ *MISCELLANEOUS.*

As much . . . as: **tanto . . . quanto.**

Egli è tanto allegro quanto suo figlio, *He is as
happy as his son.*

Io ho tanti libri quanto lei, *I have as many books
as you.*

Tale . . . quale: *just as . . ., in such condition as.*

Le penne tali quali le ho ricevute, *The pens just
as I received them.*

NUMBERS

1. uno, a.[1]	31. trentuno.
2. due.	32. trentadue.
3. tre.	33. trentatrè, etc.
4. quattro.	40. quaranta.
5. cinque.	50. cinquanta.
6. sei.	60. sessanta.
7. sette	70. settanta.
8. otto.	80. ottanta.
9. nove.	90. novanta.
10. dieci.	100. cento.
11. úndici.	101. centuno.
12. dódici.	102. centodue.
13. trédici.	200. duecento.
14. quattórdici.	300. trecento.
15. quíndici.	400. quattrocento.
16. sédici.	500. cinquecento.
17. diciassette.	600. seicento.
18. diciotto.	700. settecento.
19. diciannove.	800. ottocento.
20. venti.	900. novecento.
21. ventuno.	1000. mille.
22. ventidue.	2000. duemila.
23. ventitrè, etc.	One million,
30. trenta.	un milione.

¶ ORDINALS.

1st. **primo, a.**	6th. **sesto, a.**
2nd. **secondo, a.**	7th. **séttimo, a.**
3rd. **terzo, a.**	8th. **ottavo, a.**
4th. **quarto, a.**	9th. **nono, a.**
5th. **quinto, a**	10th. **décimo, a.**

[1] **Uno** is used in counting or before **s** impure or **z**. **Un** is the ordinary masculine form for *one*. Thus: **Un generale,** means either *a general* or *one general*.

These need not be learnt on a first perusal :—

11th.	undicesimo, a[1] (or decimoprimo, decimaprima, or undecimo, a).	33rd.	trentatreesimo, a.
		40th.	quarantesimo, a.
		50th.	cinquantesimo, a.
		60th.	sessantesimo, a.
12th.	dodicesimo, a (or decimosecondo, decimaseconda, etc.	70th.	settantesimo, a.
		80th.	ottantesimo, a.
		90th.	novantesimo, a.
		100th.	centesimo, a.
13th.	tredicesimo, a.	101st.	centunesimo, a.
14th.	quattordicesimo, a.	102nd.	centoduesimo, a.
		200th.	duecentesimo, a.
15th.	quindicesimo, a.	300th.	trecentesimo, a.
16th.	sedicesimo, a.	400th.	quattrocentesimo, a.
17th.	diciassettesimo, a.		
18th.	diciottesimo, a.	500th.	cinquecentesimo, a.
19th.	diciannovesimo, a.		
20th.	ventesimo, a.	600th.	seicentesimo, a.
21st.	ventunesimo, a.[2]	700th.	settecentesimo, a.
22nd.	ventiduesimo, a.	800th.	ottocentesimo, a.
23rd.	ventitreesimo, a.	900th.	novecentesimo, a.
30th.	trentesimo, a.	1000th.	millesimo, a.
31st.	trentunesimo, a.	2000th.	duemillesimo, a.
32nd.	trentaduesimo, a.	milionesimo, *millionth*.	

¶ USE OF NUMERALS.

Una: drops the last letter when the *next* word begins with a vowel: **un' amica,** *a (or one) friend;* **un'áncora,** *an anchor.* Use **uno** before s impure or **z**.

Uno, una, otto: when used to form compounds with other numbers cause the *other* numbers to drop

[1] In all these words from 11th onwards, in the ending **-ésimo**, the e is always stressed. It is not marked here, in order that the learner may become accustomed to the idea that there is no é, strictly speaking, in Italian.

[2] The alternative forms **ventésimoprimo, ventésimo-secondo,** etc., are often used, and in the opinion of some, are more elegant. But, for most practical purposes, the ordinals from 1st to 10th will be found sufficient.

their final vowel: Thus: **ventuno, -a, centuno, -a, ventotto.**

Cento has no feminine or plural, and in Tuscan drops the **-to** when preceding an unstressed syllable: **duecenquaranta.**

Mille and **milione** have plurals: **mila, milioni.**

On the 5th, 6th: **Ai cinque, ai sei.**

DATES. London, 15th January, 1938: **Londra, il 15 (di) gennaio (di) 1938.** What is the date? **Quanti ne abbiamo del mese?** It is the 8th: **Ne abbiamo otto.**

AGE: How old are you? **Quanti anni ha lei?** I am 25 years old. **ho 25 anni** (lit. I have 25 years). A year ago: **Un anno fa.** Within six months: **Fra sei mesi.** All two, all three, all four: **Tutti e due, tutti e tre, tutti e quattro.** Both brothers, both sisters: **ambedue i fratelli, ambedue le sorelle:** Each is translated by **ogni** (masc. and fem. and sing. only): **ogni casa**, every house.

¶ MISCELLANEOUS.[1]

zero, zero, nought.
un paio, a pair, a brace.

una coppia, a couple.

una dozzina, a dozen.
una ventina, a score.
una trentina, thirty or so.
la metà, the half.
un terzo, a third.
un quarto, a fourth, a quarter.

il doppio, the double.
il triplo, the triple.

una quarantina, 2 score.
una cinquantina, half a hundred.
un centinaio, a hundred or so.
un migliaio, a thousand or so.
a centinaia, by hundreds.
a migliaia, by thousands.
un quinto, a fifth.
uno ad uno, one by one.
due a due, two by two.

il quadruplo, the quadruple.
un centuplo, a hundredfold.

un trimestre, a term, quarter, (three months),
un triennio, three years period.
l'último, the last.

[1] Need not be memorised on a first perusal.

22

¶ THE TIME.

What time is it? **Che ora è?**

Noon, **Mezzogiorno** (or **mezzodì**, or **le dódici**).

Midnight, **Mezzanotte.**

One o'clock, **L'una** (also: **il tocco**).

2 o'clock, **Le due.**

A quarter past three, **Le tre e un quarto.**

Half past four, **Le quattro e mezzo.**

A quarter to five, **Le quattro e tre quarti** (*four and three quarters*).

Ten minutes to six, **Le sei meno dieci** (*six less ten*).

Five past seven, **Le sette e cinque.**

It is striking one, **Suona l'una.**

It is striking six, **Suónano le sei.**

PRONOUNS

" A pronoun is a word used instead of a noun or a noun equivalent.

¶ PERSONAL PRONOUNS.

I
Subject Pronouns
io, *I.*
tu, *thou*
egli, esso, *he* or *it* (masc.).
ella, essa, *she* or *it* (fem.)
Lei, *you* (see below).
noi, *we.*
voi, *you.*
églino, essi, *they* (masc.).
élleno, esse, *they* (fem.).

¶ OBJECT PRONOUNS.

		II Direct	III Indirect
Ist Pers. Sing.		mi, me, *me*.	mi, a me, *to me*.
2nd	,, ,,	la, lei, *you*.	le, a lei, *to you*[1]
,,	,,	ti, te, *thee*.	ti, a te, *to thee*.
Ist	,, Plur.	ci, noi, *us*.	ci, a noi, *to us*.
2nd	,, ,,	vi, voi, *you*.	vi, a voi, *to you*.
3rd	,, Sing.(m)	lo, lui, *him*.	gli, a lui, *to him*.
,,	,, (f)	la, lei, *her*.	le, a lei, *to her*.
,,	,, (m)	lo, esso, *it*.	vi ⎫ ad esso, *to it*.
,,	,, (f)	la, essa, *it*.	ci ⎭ ad essa, *to it*.
,,	Plur. (m)	li, ⎫ loro *them*	⎧ loro, a loro,
,,	,, (f)	le, ⎭	⎭ *to them*.
,,	,, (m)	li, essi, *them*.	vi ⎫ ad essi, *to them*.
,,	,, (f)	le, esse, *them*.	ci ⎭ ad esse, *to them*.
Reflexive, s. & p. ⎫ Himself, herself, ⎬ itself, themselves. ⎭		si, sè	si, a sè

In the above list the subject pronouns answer the question : *Who* or *what acted?* The direct object pronouns answer the question: Who or what was the *primary* recipient of the action ? The indirect object pronouns answer the question: Who or what was the *indirect* or *secondary* recipient of the action ?

Thus: I will tell it to him.

     I, is the *subject*,

     it, is the *direct object*,

     him, is the *indirect object*.

☛ Never forget that every Italian noun is either masculine or feminine in gender, and a corresponding gender must be used when it is replaced by a pronoun.

[1] Corresponds to **Lei,** for which see below.

Thus: **Ecco la mia casa, (essa) è molto bella.**
Here is my house, it is very beautiful.

As the Personal Pronouns (and, indeed, *all* pronouns)
are of frequent occurrence the student must memorise
them now. But note the following observations:

Egli, ella, églino, are used for *persons,* but **esso, essa,
essi, esse,** may be used for persons, animals or things.

In speaking (but not in literature) **essi** and **esse** are used
instead of **églino** and **élleno** (which tend to disappear
entirely).

YOU: The English word *You* is translated by **LEI,** and this
is followed by the verb in the Third Person Singular[1]. **LEI is**
used for both masculine and feminine. The plural form of **LEI**
is **LORO. Lei** and **Loro,** are essentially polite, *respectful*
forms.

Thus: **LEI HA,** *you have* (sing.).
LORO HANNO, *you have* (plur.)
Parla lei italiano? *Do you speak Italian?*

Tu is essentially a *familiar* form, used to address children,
intimates or relations and animals.

VOI, which before 1924 was used only when addressing a
number of people and in commercial correspondence, has
become the *general* word of the younger generation for the
English *You,* whether one person is addressed or more.

IT: The word ' it ' may often be omitted in Italian. **È vero,**
it is true. **Ha fatto?** *Have you done it?*

SELF: The word ' self ' may be added to the above pronouns
by ' **stesso** ' **lo stesso,** *I myself*; **Lei stesso,** *you yourself,
yourself,* etc. And in the fem. etc., **lo stessa. Lei stessa.** Plur.
noi stessi, loro stessi.

SÈ, Itself, third person singular and plural, reflexive, not
used in nominative, **se stesso,** *himself.*

¶ *CONJUNCTIVE PERSONAL PRONOUNS.*

So called because they precede the verb or can be
joined with it when they follow. They are:—

mi, *me, to me*; **ti,** *thee, to thee*; **lo,** *him, it* (masc.);

[1] This is because the word **Signoria** or **Eccellenza,**
Lordship or *Excellency,* is implied. Compare Spanish **Usted.**
Lei and **loro** were disapproved in 1924 and the young genera-
tion of Italians were taught to use always **tu** and **voi.**

gli, *to him;* **la,** *her, it;* **le,** *to her;* **ci** *or* **ne,** *us, to us;* **vi, you, to you,** **li** *or* **gli,** *them, to them* (masc.); **le,** *them, to them* (fem.); **si,** *himself, herself, themselves;* **loro,** *to them.*

Vi prego di darmi un fiammífero *I pray you (i.e. please) to give me a match.* **Crédimi,** *Believe me;* **Chiamátelo!** *Call him!* **Amarla,** *to love her.*

¶ POSITION OF PRONOUNS.

The conjunctive pronouns precede the verb as :—

> **Egli mi dà,** *he gives me.*
> **Io vi vedo,** *I see you.*
> **Lei mi ha dato,** *You have given me.*

☞ The Indirect precedes the Direct, when two object pronouns come together:—

> **Me lo dà,** *he gives it to me.*
> **Dateglielo,** *give it to him!*

NE follows the direct object;

LORO comes last, following the verb.

> **Egli ha detto loro,** *He has told them.*

ÉCCO: This word means *Here is* or *Here are* (*Voici,* in French.) *Here is John,* **Ecco Giovanni.**

Here I am *or* behold me		éccomi
Here he is *or* behold him		éccolo
Here she is *or* behold her	rendered	éccola
Here we are *or* behold us	by	éccoci
Here are some *or* behold some		éccone

¶ REFLEXIVE PRONOUNS.

The words **mi, ti, si, ci, vi, si** are used as Reflexive Pronouns in the conjugation of Reflexive Verbs (See page 53).

Io mi lavo, *I wash myself.*
Tu ti lavi, *Thou washest thyself.*
Egli si lava, *He washes himself.*
Noi ci laviamo, *We wash ourselves.*
Voi vi lavate, *You wash yourself, or selves.*
Essi si lAvano, *They wash themselves.*

¶ RELATIVE PRONOUNS.

A relative pronoun is one which connects the noun
or pronoun to which it refers with the part of the
sentence which follows. Thus: The man whom I know.
The house that Jack built.

Whom and *That* are relatives.

The English relative pronouns, *who, whom, which,*
and *that* are nearly always translated by the word **che.**

☛ In Italian the relative is *never* omitted, as it often
is in English.

Thus: *The letter (which) I wrote to you has not arrived,*
La léttera CHE vi ho scritto non è arrivata.

When the relative clause is considered to be as important as
the principal clause, or where greater clarity appears to be
necessary, after a preposition:
Singular: **il quale, la quale**
Plural: **i quali, le quali**
are used instead of **CHE.**

Mia sorella, la quale è in Roma, mi ha scritto una léttera
My sister, (who is) in Rome, has written me a letter.

Learn the following list of relatives:

Masculine singular	Feminine singular
Che or **il quale** (*who, which, that*)	**Che** or **la quale**
di cui, del quale (*of whom, which, that*)	**di cui, della quale**
a cui, cui, al quale (*to whom, which, that*)	**a cui, cui, alla quale**
che, cui, il quale (*whom, which*)	**che, cui, la quale**
da cui, dal quale (*from whom, which, etc.*)	**da cui, dalla quale**

27

	Plural.
Masculine and Feminine	**che**, who, which, that
	di cui, of whom, which, that
	a cui, to whom, which, that
	cui, whom, which
	da cui, from whom

Masculine Plural	Feminine Plural
i quali	**le quali**
dei quali	**delle quali**
ai quali	**alle quali**
i quali	**le quali**
dai quali	**dalle quali**

The word **CHI** is used only for persons and always in the singular—it means *he who, she who,* etc.

Chi piantò la vite fu Noè, *He who planted the vine was Noah.*

Chi parla adesso è mia cugina, *She who speaks now is my cousin* (fem.).

Chi va piano, va sano, *He who goes slowly goes surely.*

Il che, is often used to translate : *The thing which.* For instance : A says *It is very cold to-day,* and B wishing to reply *That I dislike* or *Cold is something I dislike* might say **Il che non mi piace.**

¶ *INTERROGATIVES.*

Chi? *Who?* **Che?** *What?* **Di chi?** *Of whom ?* **Di che?** *Of what?* **A chi?** *To whom?* **A che?** *To what?* **Chi?** *Whom?* **Che?** *What?* **Da chi?** *From whom?* **Da che?** *From what?* **Quale?** *Which, Which one?* (masc. and fem. sing.). **Quali?** *Which, Which ones?* (masc. and fem. plur.).

These words are used instead of **CHE** when the meaning is *Which one of two or more* as for example:—

Qual è il cappello dell'ufficiale? *Which (one of all these) is the officer's hat?*

Di questi due cavalli quale vuol lei? *Of these two horses which one do you wish?*

NOTE: Instead of **CHE** one very often says **CHE COSA**, *What thing:* **Che cosa fa?** *What are you doing?* Or simply **Cosa**, as **Cosa vende il bottegaio?** *What does the shopkeeper sell?*
Che (and sometimes **quale**) is used to express *What a* as *What a fine question!* **Che bella domanda !**
What a beutiful girl! **Che bella ragazza !**

¶ *DEMONSTRATIVE PRONOUNS.*

	Singular		Plural	
	masc.	fem.	masc.	fem.
THIS:	questo	questa	questi	queste
THAT:	quello	quella	que(ll)i	quelle

These words always agree in gender and number with the noun which follows them:

Quello è il male: *That's the misfortune.*

Questo è che io ho sentito, *This is what I have heard.*

Quella ragazza, *That girl.*

Quello non mi piace, *That does not please me.*

Quelle ragazze, *Those girls.*

When followed by a verb and a noun, **Questo** and **Quello** take the gender and number of that noun.

Questa è la mia casa, *This is my house.*

Quei sono fratelli, *Those are brothers.*

Note the abbreviations:

stamattina, *this morning* (**questa mattina**).

stasera, *this evening* (**questa sera**).

stanotte, *to-night* (**questa notte**).

29

Other demonstratives are:

CIÒ meaning *that* in a very general sense, and with **che**:

CIÒ CHE means *that which*.
I believe that which I see, **Io credo ciò che vedo**.

Used without a noun and for persons are:

COSTUI, *this man*: **COSTEI**, *this woman*.
Plural: **COSTORO**, *these people* (masc. and fem.).

COLUI, *that man*: **COLEI**, *that woman*.
Plural: **COLORO**, *those people* (masc. and fem.).

COLORO saranno puniti, *Those persons will be punished*.

Che cosa vuole costui? *What does that fellow want?*

Mi fanno ridere coloro, *They* (i.e. *those people*) *make me laugh*.

Beati coloro che muóiono nel Signore! *Blessed (are) those (people) who die in the Lord!*

NOTE: The words **COSTUI** and **COLUI** refer only to persons and, indeed, are elegant words which convey either a genuine admiration on the part of the speaker, or—in direct contrast—may convey indignation, contempt or sarcasm. **Beati coloro**, in the example given, represents a sincere feeling. But to translate into English, **Non mi parli di colui**, it would be necessary to add a word to express the element of indignation in the Italian. ' *Don't speak to me of that fellow.*' Used alone they may be expletives, representing indignation, contempt, sarcasm—or sheer admiration! For example: **Che pensa lei del Duce?** *What do you think of the Leader?* **Colui!** here might be translated : *What a man!* or, *Don't speak of him!*

Thither (to there), is translated by **CI** or **VI**.
Thence (from there), is translated by **NE**.
Va lei a casa? *Are you going home* (to your house)?
— **No, ne vengo**, *No, I am coming from there*.
È stato lei in Italia? *Have you been in Italy?*
— **No, ma vi andrò quest'anno**, *No, but I shall go there this year*.

N.B. The **-o** of **questo** is dropped before the vowel **-a**. The dropping of a vowel for euphony is, as the student will have appreciated by now, very common.

There is	} translated by	{	**c'è, v'è**
There are		{	**ci sono, vi sono**

C'è il sole oggi: *There is sun to-day*

There was { **c'era**
         c'érano

  C'era la moglie di mío fratello, *There was (present) my brother's wife.*

  (Students acquainted with French may compare Italian **NE** with French *en;* and Italian **VI** and **CI** with French *y.* And Italian **c'è, v'è** with French *il y a.*):

  Hai pensato a questa cosa? *Have you thought of this?*
  Ci ho pensato, *I have thought of it* (French: **J'y ai pensé**)

¶ POSSESSIVE PRONOUNS.

  The possessive pronouns and the possessive adjectives have the same forms in Italian which are :—

1st pers. sing.	**mío, mía miéi, míe,** *my.*
2nd „ „	**tuo, tua, tuoi, tue,** *thy.*
3rd „ „	**suo, sua, suoi, sue,** *his, her, its* (also *your*).
1st „ plur.	**nostro, nostra, nostri, nostre,** *our.*
2nd „ „	**vostro, vostra, vostri, vostre,** *your.*
3rd „ „	**loro** (for both genders) *their* (also *your*).

—the difference being that the possessive pronouns usually take the definite article before them if they refer to a thing in the singular and not to a person. Thus:

        mío fratello, *my brother.*
        il mío cappello, *my hat.*
        i miéi cappelli, *my hats.*

In the plural the article is used with both persons and things:

I miei fratelli, *my brothers,* though it is often omitted with persons: **Questi sono miei fratelli,** these are my brothers.

DI LUI and **DI LEI** are used instead of **suo, sua, suoi, sue** when there is any likelihood of ambiguity or misunderstanding—

This book is his and not hers, **Questo libro è di lui e non di lei.**

The possessive pronouns or adjectives may come after their noun, especially in exclamations :—

Amico mío! *My friend!*

Caríssimo mío! *My (very) dear fellow!*

A casa mía, *in my house;* **per conto mío,** *on my account;* **in nome mío,** *in my name;* **da parte mía,** *on my part.*

Che cappello è? *What hat is it?*

Non è il mío, è il suo, *Not mine—yours (or his).*

Il piacere è mío, *the pleasure is mine.*

NOTE.—POSSESSIVE PRONOUNS AND ADJECTIVES IN ITALIAN AGREE IN GENDER AND NUMBER WITH THE OBJECT POSSESSED.

¶ *INDEFINITE AND MISCELLANEOUS.*

A number of useful and frequently recurring words come under this head and must be memorised though not necessarily on a first perusal of this book. Except the ' Invariables ' given below, they must agree in gender and number with their nouns, or the nouns whose place they take.

¶ *INVARIABLES:*

OGNI, *each, every.* **Ogni giorno,** *every day.*

NIENTE, *nothing.* **Niente è inUtile,** *nothing is useless.*

NULLA, *nothing,* **Nulla ci conforta,** *nothing comforts us.*

QUALCHE, *any,* **Qualche cosa,** *anything.*

When **niente** and **nulla** follow a verb, the word **non** must be placed before the verb :—

Non c'è niente, *there is nothing.*

When they are followed by an adjective they take **DI**

When they are followed by a verb they take **DA**

Niente di buono, *nothing good.*

Niente (or **nulla**) **da dire,** *nothing to say.*

QUALUNQUE: means *any . . . whatever.*

Qualunque casa, *any house whatever.*

PER QUANTO: *however, whatever.*

Per quanto è in mio potere, *whatever is in my power.*

¶ *VARIABLES:*—

ALTRO-a-i-e: *other, another.*

ALCUNO-a-i-e, *someone, anyone.*

CIASCUNO-a, *each one, every one* (sing. only).

TUTTO-a-i-e, *all, the whole of* (**Tutti,** *everybody*).

N.B.—**TUTTO** is also used for *everything.*

NESSUNO-a, *no one.*

OGNUNO-a, *each one, every one.*

CERTUNO-a, *a certain one, one*

33

TALUNO-a-i-e, somebody, someone.

QUALCUNO-a
QUALCHEDUNO-a } someone, somebody.

TALE-i, such a one, such (**un tale,** a certain man).

TUTTO QUANTO, tutta quanta, tutti quanti, tutte quante, all, the whole (**Io ho veduto tutti quanti gli uómini:** I have seen all the men—i.e. together).

TANTO-a-i-e, so much **QUANTO -a-i-e,** how much.

L'UN L'ALTRO, L'UNA L'ALTRA; GLI UNI GLI ALTRI, LE UNE LE ALTRE, each one, one another

Ci amiamo l'un l'altro, we love one another.

Examples:
Ogni città, each town; **ogni volta,** each time; **ogni dove,** everywhere. N.B. **Ognora,** always, **Ognuno lo dice,** everybody says so (i.e. it); **ciascuna volta,** each time; **Conosce lei alcuno?** Do you know anybody? **Noi altri Inglesi,** We English (Nous autres Anglais); **Cosí fan tutte,** so all (women) do; **Tutti loro,** all of you[1]; **Quanto c'è da pagare?** How much is to be paid? **È tutt'altra cosa,** It is quite another matter; **Tutt'altró,** on the contrary; **Il signor tale mi disse,** Mr. so-and-so told me; **Il tal libro,** such a book.

NOTE ALSO: **AMBO,** both. Plur. **ambi.**

PARECCHI, PARECCHIE (masc. and fem. plur. only) several.

PIÙ D'UN, more than one, many a.

UN TANTO LA SETTIMANA, so much a week.

QUANTO PRIMA, as soon (early) as possible.

QUANTO C'È da Roma a Parigi? How far is it from Rome to Paris?

[1] You, in the polite form.

Some, a certain, one	Each, every	Anybody
uno **un certo** **un tale** **certuno** **taluno**	**ogni*** **ognuno** **ciascuno** **tutto**	**alcuno** **qualcuno** **qualche*** **qualcheduno**
Who what } ever how	No-one none nobody	Other another
qualunque*	**nullo** **nulla*** **niente*** **nessuno**	**altro**

NOTE.—The words in this table are of frequent recurrence and must be known. The equivalents above are approximate—those in the text should be memorised.

¶ THE WORD SI.

The word **SI** presents some difficulties which may conveniently be treated here. It has the following meanings in Italian:—

Sì—(1) *Yes.*

Sì—(2) *So, so much, as much.*

Si—(3) *One's self* (reflexive pronoun, see page 26).

* Invariable, the remainder variable.

35

Si—(4) Indefinite pronoun meaning *people, one, they,* (French *On*).

Si—(5) to form the passive (see page 50).

Examples:—

(1) **Parla lei inglese? Sì signore,** *Do you speak English. Yes Sir.*

(2) **Ella canta sì dolcemente,** *She sings so sweetly.* **Sì nella religione che nella política,** *As much in religion as in politics.*

(3) **Egli si lava,** *He washes himself.*

(4) **Si mangia quando si ha fame,** *One eats when one is hungry.*

(5) **Se si sa, non si dice,** *If it is known, it is not said.*

AND NOTE.—**SE** means *if* and **Si** is also the conjunctive pronoun (see page 26).

VERBS

" A verb is a word used for saying something about some person or thing."

Compared with the verbs of some other languages (Russian for example) those of Italian are straightforward. In Italian the student may gain assurance from the knowledge that:—

(*a*) He need not learn all the parts of even regular verbs—unless he wishes to become an expert translator, or until he has achieved a fair working acquaintance with the language.

(*b*) The essential verbs of the first conjugation (ending **-ARE**) are very numerous, and are *all regular except four,* these four being easy to learn and very useful. (See pages 61–3).

(c) The irregular verbs of most frequent occurrence number less than 100 and of these it is necessary to learn only the most useful tenses, as given in the following pages.

The treatment of the verb here is highly simplified, and the student must realise from the outset that (unless otherwise noted) he cannot afford to neglect any of it. What is given must ultimately be known thoroughly.

☛ The best way to learn the verbs is first to read through these pages a few times in order to grasp the general principles—no need to memorise to begin with. When the principles are understood, then **ESSERE** and **AVERE** must be learnt thoroughly; then the 'Models' for the regular conjugations; then the Irregular verbs in *large type;* and finally the remainder of the irregulars.

¶ *PARTS OF THE VERB WHICH MUST BE KNOWN.*

(a) *The Infinitive,* i.e. that part of a verb which names the action, without reference to any doer, and is therefore not limited by person, number or time. Thus: **PORTARE,** *to carry* or *bring;* **CREDERE,** *to believe;* **DORMIRE,** *to sleep;* **FINIRE,** *to finish.*

(b) *The Present Tense,* which represents the English forms ' I —,' ' I do —,' ' I am —ing.'
Thus the word **PORTO,** the Present Tense of **Portare,** means *I carry, I do carry,* or, *I am carrying.*

(c) *The Imperfect Tense,* which is used for a continuous or habitually repeated action in the past; or for an action which is contemporaneous with another action. Thus: **PORTAVO** means, *I carried, I was carrying, I used to carry.*

37   D

(d) *The Past Definite* which, as its name indicates, represents a past action which has been completely ended and has no reference to any other action. Thus **PORTAI**, means *I carried* (*I did carry*), as for example in the sentence, I carried the cup out of the dining room (and placed it on the kitchen table).

(e) *The Future Tense* which corresponds exactly to the English ' I shall — ' Thus: *I shall carry*, **PORTERÒ**.

(f) *The Past Participle*, which usually corresponds to the similar part of speech in English ending in -ed, or -t and is used with an auxiliary verb to form compound tenses, of which the most frequently recurring in Italian is generally called the ' Perfect.' Thus: **Io ho portato,** *I have carried* (**PORTATO** is the Past Participle).

General Rule for Conjugation.—All verbs ending in **-ARE** are conjugated like **PORTARE**: all verbs ending in **-ERE** are conjugated like **CREDERE**; all verbs ending in **-IRE** are conjugated like either **DORMIRE** or **FINIRE**. Those which do not follow the models of these four verbs (see below) are called irregular. Their essential parts will be found on pages 59–82.

¶ *FORMATION OF TENSES.*

For purposes of reference a complete table of the inflexions of regular verbs is given on page 41. Every part of a regular verb can be formed from this table, but there are certain principles of tense-formation which should be known.

(1) When the infinitive ending **-ARE, -ERE** or **-IRE** is dropped, the part remaining is called the *stem*. Thus:—

PORT- is the stem of **PORTARE**
CRED- „ „ „ „ **CREDERE**
DORM-„ „ „ „ **DORMIRE**
FIN- „ „ „ „ **FINIRE**

☞ IT IS TO THIS STEM THAT THE ENDINGS GIVEN IN THE TABLE ON PAGE 41 ARE ADDED TO FORM THE VARIOUS TENSES.

(2) The Present Indicative is formed by adding the following endings to the Stem.

Singular

	1st Person	2nd Person	3rd Person
Verbs in -**ARE**	-**O**	-**I**	-**A**
„ „ -**ERE**	-**O**	-**I**	-**E**
„ „ -**IRE**	-**O**	-**I**	-**E**
„ „ -**IRE**	(-isc)**O**	(-isc)**I**	(-isc)**E**

Plural

	1st Person	2nd Person	3rd Person
Verbs in -**ARE**	-**IAMO**	-**ATE**	-**ANO**
„ „ -**ERE**	-**IAMO**	-**ETE**	-**ONO**
„ „ -**IRE**	-**IAMO**	-**ITE**	-**ONO**
„ „ -**IRE**	-**IAMO**	-**ITE**	(-ísc)**ONO**

(3) The Imperfect Tense of all regular verbs is formed by adding the following endings to the stem:—

-**VO** -**VI** -**VA** -**VAMO** -**VATE** -**VANO**

N.B.—The Imperfect Tense is very rarely irregular. There is an old form for the 1st person singular ending in -**VA,** which is still often used in writing.

(4) The Past Definite is formed by adding to the Stem, the endings :
Verbs in :—

-ARE: -AI -ASTI -Ò -AMMO -ASTE -ARONO
-ERE: -EI -ESTI -È -EMMO -ESTE -ERONO
-IRE: -II -ISTI -Ì -IMMO -ISTE -IRONO

(5) The Future Tense of all regular verbs is formed by adding to the infinitive from which **-E** has been dropped, the following :—

-Ò -AI -A -EMO -ETE -ANNO

and the **-AR** is changed into **-er**. Thus: **parlare,** *to speak.* Fut: **parlerò.**

(6) The *Conditional Tense* is formed by adding to the infinitive from which **-E** has been dropped the following:

-EI -ESTI -EBBE -EMMO -ESTE -EBBERO

It will be observed that (excepting the first) these endings are the Past Definite of **Avere.**

(7) The polite form of the Imperative is always the Third Person of the Present Subjunctive and ends as follows:—

Verbs in -ARE:	-I	(singular)	-INO (plural)
,, ,, -ERE:	-A		-ANO
,, ,, -IRE	-A		-ANO
,, ,, -IRE:	(ísc)A		(-ísc)ANO

THE ENDINGS OF ITALIAN VERBS INDICATE THE PERSON AND NUMBER SO CLEARLY THAT PRONOUNS MAY GENERALLY BE OMITTED. BUT PRONOUNS SHOULD ALWAYS BE USED FOR EMPHASIS OR TO AVOID AMBIGUITY. Thus. **Porto,** *I carry.* **Portai,** *I carried.* **Io porto,** *It is I who carry.*

¶ TABLE OF INFLEXIONS OF REGULAR VERBS.

Verbs in -ARE (Port-)

Present	Imp.	Pres. Subj.	Imperfect	Future	Conditional	Past Def.	Perf. Subj.
-o		-i	-Avo, Ava	-erò	-erEi	-Ai	-Assi
-i	-a	-i	-Avi	-erAi	-erEsti	-Asti	-Assi
-a	-i	-i	-Ava	-erÀ	-erEbbe	-ò	-Asse
-iAmo	-iAmo	-iAmo	-avAmo	-erEmo	-erEmmo	-Ammo	-Assimo
-Ate	-Ate	-iAte	-avAte	-erEte	-erEste	-Aste	-Aste
-ano	-ino	-ino	-Avano	-erAnno	-erEbbero	-Arono	-Assero

Verbs in -ERE (cred-)

Present	Imp.	Pres. Subj.	Imperfect	Future	Conditional	Past Def.	Perf. Subj.
-o		-a	-evo-Eva	-erò	-erEi	-Ei	-Essi
-i	-i	-a	-Evi	-erAi	-erEsti	-Esti	-Essi
-e		-a	-Eva	-erÀ	-erEbbe	-è	-Esse
-iAmo	-iAmo	-iAmo	-evAmo	-erEmo	-erEmmo	-emmo	-Essimo
-Ete	-Ete	-iate	-evAte	-erEte	-erEste	-Este	-Este
-ono	-ano	-ano	-Evano	-erAnno	-erEbbero	-Erono	-Essero

Verbs in -IRE (dorm-)

Present	Imp.	Pres. Subj.	Imperfect	Future	Conditional	Past Def.	Perf. Subj.
-o		-a	-Ivo, Iva	-irò	-irEi	-ii	-Issi
-i	-i	-a	-Ivi	-irAi	-irEsti	-Isti	-Issi
-e		-a	-Iva	-irà	-irEbbe	-ì	-Isse
-iAmo	-iAmo	-iAmo	-ivAmo	-irEmo	-irEmo	-immo	-Issìmo
-ìte	-ìte	-iAte	-ivAte	-irEte	-irEste	-Iste	-iste
-ono	-ano	-ano	-Ivano	-irAnno	-irEbbero	-Irono	-Issero

GERUNDS : PortANDO, CredENDO, DormENDO

PAST PARTICIPLES : PortATO, CredUTO, DormITO.

NOTE.—In the above table, the stress is marked by a capital letter or an acute accent only to indicate the stressed syllable—it is never written; the grave accent (ˋ) is always written. Note the participle endings.

41

¶ WHAT THE VARIOUS ITALIAN TENSES REPRESENT IN ENGLISH.

Let us take the regular verb **PARLARE**. to speak, conjugated exactly like **PORTARE**, and, in the first person of each tense, the translation would be: —

Infinitive: **PARLARE**, to speak.
Pres. Part.: **Parlando**, speaking.
Past Part.: **Parlato**, spoken.

Indicative: —

Pres. tense: **Parlo**, I speak, I am speaking, I do speak.
Imperfect: **Parlavo**, I spoke (was speaking); (also, I used to speak).
Past Def. **Parlai**, I spoke (once, on one occasion); did speak.
Future: **Parlerò**, I shall speak.
Conditional: **Parlerei**, I should speak.

Imperative: —

Parla, speak thou; **parli**, let him speak (also polite, speak you).

Subjunctive: —

Present: **Che io parli**, that I speak.
Imperfect: **Che io parlassi**, that I spoke (**Se io parlassi**, if I spoke).

Compound Tenses: —

Perfect: **Ho parlato**, I have spoken.
1st Pluperf.: **Avevo parlato**, I had spoken (been speaking)
2nd Pluperf.: **Ebbi parlato**, I had spoken
Future Perf.: **Avrò parlato**, I shall have spoken.
Past Conditional: **Avrei parlato**, I should have spoken.

And similarly, Subjunctive compound tenses: —

Perfect: **Ch'io abbia parlato**, that I have spoken.
Pluperfect: **Ch'io (se io) avessi parlato**, that (if) I had spoken; or, had I spoken.

NOTE. —For the auxiliary **AVERE** used in forming these compound tenses, see page 44.

N.B.—Neither the table of inflexions (page 41) nor the above need be memorised at this stage. The somewhat extended treatment is given so that when the student shall have acquired some working vocabulary, he may be able to return here for guidance. Yet, it is advisable to read and re-read these pages until the general principles are grasped. Once grasped, they are easily memorised. This does not apply to the auxiliary verbs **AVERE** and **ESSERE**, which must be mastered NOW!

¶ THE GERUND

The student will often meet the Gerund in speaking or reading. It ends in **-ANDO** for **-ARE** verbs and **-ENDO** for all others; and is invariable. It corresponds to the English Present Participle in **-ing**, and has many other uses which may be avoided until the language is familiar. It is often used with the verb **STARE** to represent the English continuous present, as:

Sto aspettando, *I am waiting.*

Also note the use:

ESSENDO ammalato non posso andare— *Being ill, I cannot go.*

The beginner should be able to recognise it, but on the whole it is better to give it a miss, as the usage is rather subtle. The true Present Participle is not much in use, and may be ignored.

¶ THE AUXILIARY VERBS.

AVERE, to have. Present Participle, avendo. Past Participle, avuto.

Pres. Indic.	Imper- fect	Past Def.	Future	Condit- ional	Imper- ative	Pres- subj.	Imperfect subj.
ho	avevo	ebbi	avrò	avrei		che io abbia	se io avessi
hai	avevi	avesti	avrai	avresti	abbi	che tu abbia	se tu avessi
ha	aveva	ebbe	avrà	avrebbe	abbia	che egli abbia	se egli avessi
abbiamo	avevamo	avemmo	avremo	avremmo	abbia- mo	che noi abbiamo	se noi avessimo
avete	avevate	aveste	avrete	avreste	abbiate	che voi abbiate	se voi aveste
hanno	avEvano	ébbero	avranno	avrEbbe- ro	abbiano	che essi, esse ábbiano	se essi avEssero

ESSERE,[1] to be. Present Participle, essendo. Past Participle, stato.

sono	ero	fui	sarò	sarei		che io sia	se io fossi
sei	eri	fosti	sarai	saresti	sii	che tu sia	se tu fossi
è	era	fu	sarà	sarebbe	sia	che egli sia	se egli fosse
siamo	eravamo	fummo	saremo	saremmo	siamo	che noi siamo	se noi fossimo
siete	eravate	foste	sarete	sareste	siate	che voi siate	se voi foste
sono	érano	fúrono	saranno	sarEb- bero	siano	che essi síano	se essi fOssero

NOTE.—By referring to Page 42 the student should quickly master what the above represent.

[1] See next page.

44

ESSERE in its compound tenses is conjugated with itself, and not with 'to have' as in English. Thus, *I have been* is **Io sono stato**; *I had been,* **Io ero stato,** and so on throughout.

RULE.—Use **ESSERE** to form the compound tenses of all intransitive verbs and **AVERE** for transitive. Thus:

> **Esso è morto,** *He has died.*
> **Io ho amato,** *I have loved.*

(A verb is said to be *transitive* when its action is directed towards some person or thing, and does not stop within itself : *I hit John,* ' hit ' is a transitive verb. But when the action or feeling is not directed towards something else, and stops within itself, the verb is said to be *intransitive*. Thus *Rivers flow ; Mary sleeps ; Men die.* ' flow ',' sleeps ', ' die ', are intransitive verbs).

¶ *MODELS FOR ESSENTIAL TENSES.*

(1) Regular verbs.

Infin. :	**PORTARE,** *to carry ;* **CREDERE,** *to believe ;* **DORMIRE,** *to sleep.*
Pres. Part. :	**PORTANDO, CREDENDO, DORMENDO.**
Past. Part. :	**PORTATO, CREDUTO, DORMITO.**
Pres. Tense :	**Porto, porti, porta, portiamo, portate, pórtano.**
	Credo, credi, crede, crediamo, credete, crédono.
	Dormo, dormi, dorme, dormiamo, dormite, dórmono.
Imperfect :	**Portavo, credevo, dormivo,** etc.
Past Def. :	**Portai, credei, dormii,** etc.
Future :	**Porterò, crederò, dormirò.**

(2) Irregular Verbs.

IN THE LISTS OF IRREGULAR VERBS ON PAGES 61—82 THE INFINITIVE, THE PRESENT, THE PAST DEFINITE AND THE PAST PARTICIPLE, BEING THE ESSENTIAL PARTS FROM WHICH ALL OTHERS MAY BE FORMED, ARE GIVEN. ALSO OTHER ESSENTIAL PARTS WHICH MAY BE IRREGULAR— THE FUTURE OR PRESENT SUBJUNCTIVE, FOR EXAMPLE, AS FROM THE LATTER THE IMPERATIVE IS FORMED. IT MAY BE ASSUMED THAT OTHERWISE THE VERB IS REGULAR OR THAT ANY OTHER IRREGULARITIES MAY BE IGNORED AS NOT OF FREQUENT OCCURRENCE.

¶ *ORTHOGRAPHIC CHANGES FOR EUPHONY.*

When the infinitive ending **-ARE** is preceded : by **c** or **g,** these letters retain the hard sound *all through the verb,* as **io tronco,** *I cut off,* **noi troncheremo,** *we shall cut off,* **voi tronchiate,** *that you may cut off;* **io pago,** *I pay,* **noi pagheremo,** *we shall pay,* **voi paghiate,** *that you pay.*

—by **i,** this vowel is retained when it comes before another, but it is dropped before *all* terminations beginning with **i,** as : **io conio,** *I coin,* **noi coniamo,** *we coin,* **essi cónino,** *that they coin.*

When the stress is on the **-i,** this vowel must be retained all through the verb : **io spío,** *I spy,* **tu spíi,** *thou spiest,* **essi spíino** *that they spy.*

When the infinitive ending is preceded by **ci-, gi-,** the vowel **i** is retained through all tenses, except when the termination begins with **i** or **e.** Example : **Io rintraccio,** *I investigate,* **essi rintráccino,** *that they investigate;* **voi rintraccerete,** *you will investigate;* **Io passeggio,** *I walk;* **essi passéggino,** *that they walk;* **voi passeggerete,** *you will walk.*

Infinitives which end in **-gnare** omit **i** from the ending **-iamo. Bisognare,** *to require;* **bisognamo,** *we require.*

When the termination **-ERE** (unaccented) is preceded by **c** or **g,** both these consonants preserve the soft sound before the vowels **e** and **i;** but they take the hard sound before the vowels **a** and **o.**

Thus from the verb **torcere,** *to twist;* **egli torc-e,** *he twists;* but **io torc-o,** *I twist;* **che essi tórc-ano,** *that they twist;* from **pungere,** *to prick;* **egli pung-e,** *he pricks;* but **io pung-o,** *I prick;* **che essi púng-ano,** *that they prick.*

¶ *NOTE ON VERBS ENDING –IRE.*

Although **DORMIRE,** *to sleep,* represents a regular verb ending -**IRE,** a comparatively small number of verbs follow the rules for regular conjugation as given in the Table of Inflections (page 41) and the Models (page 45) for **DORMIRE.** But the small group which follows **DORMIRE** is important, and is therefore given here for convenience. Those verbs in large type are essential and must be memorized now : The full list is :

AVVERTIRE, *to warn*	**PENTIRSI,** *to repent*
BOLLIRE, *to boil*	**Pervertire,** *to pervert*
CONVERTIRE, *to convert*	**SEGUIRE,** *to follow*
Cucire, *to sew*	**SENTIRE,** *to feel*
Divertire, *to amuse*	**Tossire,** *to cough*
DORMIRE, *to sleep*	**VESTIRE,** *to dress*
Fuggire, *to flee*	**Travestire,** *to disguise*
PARTIRE, *to depart, leave.*	

¶ *FREQUENTATIVE VERBS IN* -**IRE.**

By far the greatest number of verbs ending in -**IRE** take -*isc-* *between the stem and the endings* given in the Table of Inflexions on page 41, but only in some persons of the Present, the Present Subjunctive, and consequently the Imperative. Take for example, the essential verb **FINIRE,** *to finish :*

FINIRE, *to finish;* **FINENDO,** *finishing;* **FINITO,** *finished.*

Present:	**FINISCO, FINISCI, FINISCE,** finiamo, finite, **FINÍSCONO.**
Imperf:	**Finivo,** etc.
Past Def.:	**Finii,** etc.
Future:	**Finirò,** etc.

Pres. Subj.: **Che io FINISCA, tu FINISCA, egli FINISCA, noi finiamo, voi finiate, essi FINÍSCANO.**

Imperative: **FINISCA** (Polite form) *Finish!* Plural: **FINÍSCANO.**

These **-isc-** verbs are called " Frequentative " in Italian.

RULE.—ALL **-IRE** VERBS WHICH ARE NEITHER IRREGULAR NOR CONJUGATED LIKE **DORMIRE** (see list above) ARE CONJUGATED LIKE **FINIRE.**

¶ *LIST OF VERBS CONJUGATED LIKE FINIRE.*

The following list is given for convenience. The verbs in large type should be mastered as soon as possible. These **DORMIRE** AND **FINIRE** verbs together with the few irregular **-IRE** verbs given later (pages 75–7) represent the most frequently recurring verbs of this conjugation.

VERBS WITH THE INFLEXION -ÍSC-

aborrire, *abhor.*
addolcire, *sweeten.*
AGIRE, *act.*
alleggerire, *lighten.*
allestire, *prepare.*
ambire, *desire ardently, covet.*
ammonire, *admonish.*
ardire, *dare.*
asserire, *assert.*
assordire, *deafen.*
atterire, *terrify.*
attribuire, *attribute.*
avvilire, *abase.*
CAPIRE, *understand.*
colorire, *colour.*
colpire, *strike.*
compatire, *pity.*
concepire, *conceive.*
conferire, *confer.*

CONTRIBUÍRE, *contribute.*
COSTRUIRE, *construct.*
DEFINIRE, *define.*
demolire, *demolish.*
DIFFERIRE, *differ.*
digerire, *digest.*
DIMINUIRE, *diminish.*
DISOBBEDIRE, *disobey.*
DISUNIRE, *separate.*
esaurire, *exhaust.*
FALLIRE, *fail.*
favorire, *favour.*
ferire, *wound.*
fiorire, *blossom, flourish.*
FORNIRE, *furnish.*
fruíre, *enjoy the fruits of.*
GARANTIRE, *guarantee.*
impallidire, *grow pale.*
IMPAURIRE, *frighten.*

48

IMPEDIRE, hinder.
incivilire, civilise.
INDEBOLIRE, weaken.
INFASTIDIRE, annoy.
ingelosire, grow jealous.
ingrandire, grow taller.
insuperbire, grow proud.
intimorire, grow fearful.
ISTRUIRE, instruct.
muggire, bellow, howl.
munire, provide (with).
OBBEDIRE, obey.
PREFERIRE, prefer.
presagire, prognosticate.
progredire, advance, make progress.
PROIBIRE, prohibit.
PERSEGUIRE, pursue.
PULIRE, clean.
PUNIRE, punish.
RESTITUIRE, restore.
ripulire, polish, clean.

riverire, respect, revere.
ruggire, roar.
scolorire, fade, lose colour.
seppellire, bury.
SMARRIRE, lose, mislead.
SMENTIRE, contradict.
SOSTITUIRE, substitute.
SPARIRE, disappear.
SPEDIRE, dispatch.
STABILIRE, establish.
starnutire, sneeze.
gradire, accept.
GUARIRE, cure.
guarnire, trim, furnish.
STUPIRE, to be amazed.
suggerire, suggest.
SUPPLIRE, supply.
SVANIRE, vanish.
tradire, betray.
trasferire, remove.
trasgredire, transgress.
UNIRE, unite.

¶ VERBS IN -IRE LIKE **DORMIRE** OR **FINIRE**.

There are some verbs which may be conjugated like either **DORMIRE** or **FINIRE**:

APPLAUDIRE, to applaud: applaudo or applaudisco.
AVVERTIRE, to warn: avverto or avvertisco (rare).
BOLLIRE, to boil: bollo or bollisco (rare).
SPARTIRE, divide: sparto or spartisco.
INVERTIRE, invert: inverto or invertisco.
MENTIRE, to tell lies: mento or mentisco.
NUTRIRE, to nourish: nutro or nutrisco.

NOTE.—Apparire, to appear; **APPAIO** or **APPARISCO**, I appear; **PARTIRE,** to depart, leave; **Io parto,** I set off; but **Io spartisco** means I divide; **DIVERTIRE** means both to amuse or to divert; **Io diverto,** I amuse.

¶ THE PASSIVE OF VERBS.

The Passive is formed in Italian as in English by using the verb *to be* (**ESSERE**) in the mood, tense and person required, with the Past Participle of the verb of which the Passive is required. Thus: *I am praised*, **Sono lodato** (From **LODARE**, *to praise*).

The Past Participle in Italian agrees in Gender and Number with the subject to which it refers: Thus:—

> **È lodato** means *he is praised*.
> **È lodata** means *she is praised*.
> **Sono lodati** means *They* (i.e. men) *are praised*.
> **Sono lodate** means *they* (women) *are praised*.
> **Siamo lodati** means *we are praised* (men) etc.

CHIAMARE, *to call;* **ESSERE CHIAMATO**, *to be called.*

Present:	**io sono chiamato**,	*I am called.*
Imperfect:	**io ero** or **era chiamato**,	*I was called.*
Past Def.:	**io fui chiamato**,	*I was called.*
Future:	**Io sarò chiamato**,	*I shall be called.*
Condit.:	**io sarei chiamato**,	*I should be called.*
Imperative:	**sii** (**tu**) **chiamato**,	*be called.*

The student should now understand:—

io sono stato chiamato, *I have been called.*
io ero or **era stato chiamato**, *I have been called.*
io fui chiamato, *I had been called.*
io sarò stato chiamato, *I shall have been called.*
io sarei stato chiamato, *I should have been called.*
(**che**) **io sia chiamato**, (*that*) *I be called.*
(**che**) **io fossi chiamato**, (*that*) *I were called.*
(**che**) **io sia stato chiamato**, (*that*) *I have been called.*
(**che**) **io fossi stato chiamato**, (*that*) *I had been called.*
éssere stato, -a, -i, -e, chiamato, -a, -i, -e, *to have been called.*

50

essendo stato, -a, -i, -e, chiamato, -a, -i, -e,
having been called.

stato, -a, -i, -e, chiamato, -a, -i, -e, *(having) been called.*

VENIRE, *to come,* is often used instead of **ESSERE** in the simple tenses of the passive, but in the compound **ESSERE** must always be used: **Vengo (or sono) punito,** *I am punished;* **Vengo (or sono) chiamato,** *I am called.* But: **Sono stato punito,** *I have been punished.*

The passive is also (and very frequently) expressed by the Reflexive (for which see below):

Come si pronunzia questa parola? *How is this*
or *word*
Come è pronunziata questa parola? *pronounced?*
Si parla italiano, *Italian (is) spoken.*
Si dice, *It is said, people say* (French: *On dit*).

The compound tenses of this Reflexive Passive are formed with **ESSERE:**—

Si è parlato italiano, *Italian was* (has been) *spoken.*

Si è detto che avremo la guerra, *It has been said that we shall have war.*

Vietare, *to prohibit.* **È vietato di fumare**
È stato vietato di fumare.

BY after a Passive must be rendered by **DA: Io sono amato da mia madre,** *I am loved by my mother.*

¶ *REFLEXIVE VERBS.*

A verb is called reflexive when (*a*) the action is performed and suffered by the subject and (*b*) when two personal pronouns instead of one are used in conjugation in order to express the action. In English

comparatively few verbs are reflexive, but the reflexive form is common in Italian; though the Italian
need not necessarily be translated by the English
reflexive. Thus : **Vestirsi**, *to dress oneself*, is a
reflexive verb in both languages, but **PENTIRSI**
means to *repent*, and is by its nature reflexive in
Italian: **Io mi pento**, *I repent*. There is no difference
in the conjugation of the Italian verbs which are
naturally reflexive and those which are obviously
reflexive in both languages.

LAVARSI, *to wash oneself.*
io mi lavo, *I wash myself.*
tu ti lavi, *thou washest thyself.*
egli si lava, *he washes himself.*
noi ci laviamo, *we wash ourselves.*
voi vi lavate, *you wash yourselves.*
essi si lávano, *they wash themselves.*
io mi lavavo, *I washed myself, or was washing
  myself.*
io mi lavai, *I washed myself.*

io mi laverò, *I shall wash myself.*
io mi laverei, *I should wash myself.*

lAvati, *wash thyself.*
si lavi, *let him wash himself.* **Si lavi,** *wash yourself*
  (polite).
laviAmoci, *let us wash ourselves.*
lavAtevi, *wash yourselves.*
si lAvino, *let them wash themselves (yourselves).*

io mi sono lavato, *I have washed myself etc.*

io mi ero or **era lavato,** *I had washed myself.*
io mi sarò lavato, *I shall have washed myself.*
io mi sarei lavato, *I should have washed myself.*
(che) io mi lavi, *(that) I wash myself etc.*
(che) io mi lavassi *(that) I washed myself.*

lavándosi, *washing oneself.*
(che) io mi sia lavato (that) *I have washed myself.*
(che) Io mi fossi lavato (that) *I had washed myself.*
éssersi lavato, -a, -i, -e, *to have washed oneself.*
essendosi lavato, -a, -e, -i, *having washed oneself.*

Similarly—

**Mi pento, ti penti, si pente, ci pentiamo,
vi pentite, si pEntono,** *I repent,* etc.

NOTE.—The auxiliary **ESSERE** is used to form the compound tenses of Reflexive verbs: **Io mi sono lavato; Io mi sono pentito**—*I have washed myself, I have repented.*

¶ *USEFUL ITALIAN REFLEXIVE VERBS ARE:—*

to *boast,* **vantarsi.**
to *complain,* **lagnarsi.**
to *congratulate,* **rallegrarsi (con).**
to *faint away,* **svenirsi.**
to *get angry,* **inquietarsi.**
to *get weary,* **annoiarsi.**
to *go away,* **ANDARSENE.**
to *go to bed,* **coricarsi.**
to *laugh at,* **burlarsi (di).**
to *make haste,* **affrettarsi (a).**
to *fall asleep,* **ADDORMENTARSI.**
to *fall in love with,* **innamorarsi (di).**
to *fancy,* **IMMAGINARSI (di).**
to *remember,* **ricordarsi (di).**
to *resign,* **dimettersi (da).**
to *shave,* **radersi.**
to *stop,* **fermarsi.**
to *take leave,* **congedarsi (da).**
to *trust,* **FIDARSI (di).**
to *wonder* (at), **SORPRENDERSI.
MARAVIGLIARSI (di).**

53

E

> *to be conceited,* **pretendersi.**
> *to forget,* **DIMENTICARSI.**
> *to fall sick,* **AMMALARSI.**
> *to rest,* **RIPOSARSI.**
> *to be ashamed,* **VERGOGNARSI.**
> *to get married,* **MARITARSI.**
> *to be well, unwell,* **SENTIRSI BENE, MALE.**

Note that most of these end in **-ARE.**

Examples of reflexives:—

> *What is your name?* **Come si chiama lei?**
> *He has dropped his handkerchief,* **Gli è caduto il fazzoletto.**
> *What has she done to herself?* **Che cosa si è fatto?**
> *She has cut her finger,* **S'è tagliato un dito.**
> *While shaving himself, he has cut his chin,* **Nel farsi la barba.**
> **s'è tagliato il mento.**
> *I do not wonder at it,* **Non mi sorprende**
> *What do you think of it?* **Che ve ne pare?**
> *Wash your face and hands before you put on your hat,* **Lavati**
> **il viso e le mani, prima di metterti il cappello** (familiar
> form).
> *He did not take off his coat,* **Non si levò la giacca.**
> *He is very conceited,* **Se la pretende molto.**

¶ THE NEGATIVE OF VERBS.

To form the negative of any verb or part of a verb, the word **NON,** *not,* is placed before the verb, and before the auxiliary in compound tenses : **Io non ho,** *I have not;* **Io non ho avuto,** *I have not had.* **Io non parlo,** *I do not speak.* **Non ho parlato,** *I have not spoken.*

When an objective pronoun is used, then the **NON** comes before it: **Egli non mi risponde,** *he does not reply to me.* Phrases with the negative words *Nothing,* **NIENTE, NULLA;** *Nobody,* **NESSUNO;** *Never,* **MAI;** require in Italian the

---

*The verbs in large type are essential.

additional negative **NON**. *I have nothing,* **Non ho niente**; *I see nobody,* **Non veggo nessuno**; *I never finish,* **Non finisco mai**. English phrases with the negation *No* before a noun are rendered by **NON**: *I have no money,* **Non ho denaro**.

NOT AT ALL, **NON ... PUNTO**. *I have no friends at all,* **Io non ho punto amici**.

NO MORE, NO LONGER, **NON ... PIÙ**. *She has no longer (more) patience,* **Essa non ha più pazienza**.

NOT TO, before an infinitive, **DI NON**. *I told you not to do it,* **Vi dissi di non farlo**. *Not to have anything,* **Di non aver niente**. NOTE.—*Why not?* **Perchè no?** *I say not,* **Dico di no**. *I believe not,* **Credo di no**.

NEGATIVE IMPERATIVE, is expressed by **NON** placed before the positive imperative.

Thus : **Non interrompere chi parla**, *Do not interrupt the person who is speaking.* **Non dormire qui**, *Don't sleep here* (familiar). **Non parli**, *Do not speak* (polite).

¶ *TO USE THE VERB INTERROGATIVELY.*

To ask a question, place the subject pronoun after the verb. Thus: *Have I?* **Ho io?** The English ' Do you ' is also expressed by placing the pronoun after the verb. Thus: *Do you speak Italian?* **Parla lei italiano? Non io**—*Not I!*

¶ *NEGATIVE INTERROGATIVE OF VERBS.*

Place **NON** first, then the verb, then the pronoun. Thus: *Do you not speak Italian?* **Non parla lei italiano?** *Do you not understand?* **Non capisce lei?**

In Italian it is very usual to ask a question merely by modulating the voice, without changing the construction of a direct statement—a useful formula for the beginner. Thus : **Lei parla inglese?** (Do) *you speak English?* **Lei capisce bene cio che io dico?** (Do) *you understand well what I am saying?* **Il suo padre verrà?** *Your father will come.* The formula can be made more convincing by adding: **Non è vero?** *Is it not so (true).* **Lei vuole un gelato, non è vero?** *You would like to have an ice, would you not?*

¶ IMPERSONAL VERBS.

Impersonal verbs are so called because as a rule they do not refer to a person, and they are used only in the third person singular. In the list below, the essential impersonal verbs are in large type :

It lightens, **lampeggia.**
It thunders, **tuona.**
It rains, **PIOVE.**
It pours, **diluvia.**
It hails, **grandina**
It is bad weather, **fa cattivo tempo.**
It freezes, **gela.**
It thaws, **sgela.**
It snows, **nevica.**
The wind blows, **tira vento.**
It is cold, **FA FREDDO.**
It is warm, **FA CALDO.**
It is fine, **FA BEL TEMPO.**
It appears, **pare** or **sembra.**
It happens, **accade.**
I happened to, **mi accade di.**
It is proper to . . . **CONVIENE . . .**
It is necessary to, **BISOGNA.**
It ought to be, **dovrebb 'éssere.**
It matters not, **NON IMPORTA.**
It is needful, **occorre.**
I care for it, **mi preme** or **mi cale** (poet).
It is enough, **BASTA.**

56

It pleases, **PIACE.**
It begins, **COMINCIA.**
It will not be necessary, **non ci occorrerà.**
It has happened (that) **È AVVENUTO** (che).

¶ *TO TRANSLATE ' THERE IS ' ' THERE ARE.'*

The English Impersonal Verb ' *there to be* ' is expressed in the same way in Italian; **ésserci** or **ésservi,** the adverb *THERE* being **ci** or **vi**:

There is, **c'è** or **v'è.**
There are, **ci sono** or **vi sono.**
There was, **c'era** or **v'era,** or **ci fu** or **vi fu.**
There were, **c'érano** or **ci fúrono.**
There will be, **ci sarà** or **ci saranno.**
There would be, **ci sarebbe** or **ci sarEberro.**
There has been, **c'è stato-a.**
There have been, **ci sono stati-e.**
That there may be, **che ci sía** or **síano.**
That there must be, **bisogna che ci sía** or **che ci síano.**
Is there? **V'è** or **C'è?** *Was there?* **V'era** or **C'Era?**

To form the negative simply place **NON** before any of the above: **Non c'è,** *There is not.* **Non c'era,** *There was not,* etc.

¶ *THE SUBJUNCTIVE AND ITS USES (FOR REFERENCE).*

The correct use of the Subjunctive is one of the difficulties of Italian, but it may be some solace to the English learner to know, first, that only well educated Italians use it correctly, secondly that there is a tendency for it to fall out of use, and thirdly that, except when he is reading, he can by a little ingenuity avoid it altogether. Furthermore, if he should use it incorrectly in everyday speech, he will readily be forgiven by the majority of Italians, and for a very good reason: that they are never too sure of it themselves! However, the Italian subjunctive is undoubtedly of frequent occurrence, and if the student wishes to become a competent translator, he should study carefully the rules given in a good Italian Grammar written for the use

57

of Italians* that is, after he has mastered *The Basis and Essentials* —the bare bones of the language—given in this book. Unhappily for the English student he cannot hope to avoid the Subjunctive, if he wishes to appreciate the subtleties of Italian (or indeed any Latin language).

General indications.—The Italian Subjunctive is (a) the MOOD OF UNCERTAINTY and (b) it is always SUBORDINATE.

It is used after DESIRE, UNCERTAINTY, EMOTION, DENIAL, BELIEF, OPINION. Under the heading of EMOTION should come : delight, rapture, astonishment, fear, grief, dismay, entreaty. The following examples indicate the usage.

I. DESIRE : **Desiderei che venisse.** *I should like him to come.*
Chiedo ch'egli m'ubbidisca. *I wish him to obey me.*
Voglio che me lo dica. *I want him to tell me it.*
Voleva che lo vedessi. *He wished me to see him.*

UNCERTAINTY: **Credo ch'egli vada oggi,** *I think he will go to-day.*
Non c'è nessuno che lo fáccia, *There's nobody to do it.*

EMOTION: **ho paura che non venga,** *I am (very much) afraid he will not come.*
Temo che egli sía andato via, *I fear he has gone away.*
Mi sorprende che non lo sappia, *I am surprised you do not know it.*

DENIAL: **Non c'è uomo che non ábbia il suo dEbole,** *No man but has his weak point.*

BELIEF }
OPINION } **Credo che sía andato,** *I think that he has gone.*

The above exemplify the two general indications of *Uncertainty* and the *Subordinate* nature of the Subjunctive.

II. After impersonal expressions such as:
Bisogna che, *It is necessary, needful that . . .*
È necessario che *It is necessary that . . .*
È meglio che, *It is better that . . .*
Basta che, *It is sufficient that . . .*
È peccato che, *It is a pity that . . .*
Pare che, *It seems that . . .*
Bisogna che io venga domani, *I must come tomorrow.*

III. After certain conjunctions with **CHE** given in the list on pages 89–90.
Supposto che questo sía vero, *Supposing this is true.*

* **La Grammática degl'Italiani** by Trabalza and Allodoli (3rd edition, Florence 1934).

58

IV. After a Negative or Superlative:
Questa è la casa più grande ch'io abbia mai veduta, *This is the biggest house I have ever seen.*
Non c'è nessuno che capisca l'italiano, *There's nobody who understands Italian.*

V. After **PRIMO,** *first;* **SOLO, ÚNICO,** *only,* and **ÚLTIMO,** *last.*
È il primo Francese ch'io abbia conosciuto, *He is the first Frenchman I have ever known.*
Lei è l'único amico di cui possa fidarmi, *You are the only friend on whom I can rely.*

VI. After the Indefinite Pronoun **CHI** implying doubt, wonder:
Chi crede che sía? *Who do you think he is?*

VII. After adverbs and pronouns denoting something vague or doubtful :
Qualunque sía la sua sorte, *Whatever your fate (may) be.*

VIII. IF I HAD, HAD I; Translate into Italian by **SE** and the Imperfect Subjunctive followed by the second verb in the Conditional.
Se io avessi tempo anderei, *If I had time I'd go.*

RULE FOR USE OF SUBJUNCTIVE TENSES.—Use the Present Subjunctive when the first verb is in the Present or Future Indicative, otherwise use the Imperfect Subjunctive:—
Mi domandò chi fossi, *He asked me who I was.*
Io non so chi sía, *I do not know who he is.*

¶ IRREGULAR VERBS.

General remarks. The list of Italian irregular verbs may appear long, but the student will find that many irregularities follow definite rules and present little difficulty. Irregularities generally occur in the:—

Present Indicative.
Present Subjunctive.
Imperative.
Past Definite.
Past Participle.
Future and Conditional (in a few verbs only).

RULES :

(1) Past Definite irregularities occur in the 1st person singular, which ends in **i**. Also in the third person singular, which ends in **e**; and in the third person plural which adds **-ro** to the third person singular. Exceptions: **Dire, stare, fare, porre, dire**—which see. (Pages 61–63).

(2) The Imperative follows the same irregularities as the Present Subjunctive for the polite forms (and as the Present Indicative for 2nd persons).

(3) The Future and Conditional usually have the same sort of irregularity, which is often merely a slight contraction or alteration, rather than a real irregularity. Thus **andrò** instead of **anderò**.

(4) All derivative and compound verbs follow their simple verbs in irregularities. Thus: **DISFARE**, *to undo, unmake*, is conjugated exactly like **FARE**, *to do, to make*. All exceptions to this rule will be noted. [The student must use his intelligence to judge when a verb is a derivative or compound and when it is not. For example, **SOTTOSTARE** is clearly a compound of **sotto**, *underneath, below*, and **stare**, *to stand*, because it means *to be beneath, to stand beneath*: so it follows **stare**. But **COSTARE**, *to cost*, is (obviously) not related to **stare**. It is regular.]

(5) The Imperfect Indicative is always regular. Except **dare, fare, porre** (which see).

(6) The Imperfect Subjunctive is always regular. (Except ; **dare, stare, trarre**, which take **-essi** instead of **-assi**: and **dire, fare, porre** which make **dicessi, facessi, ponessi**.)

(7) Tenses which are not given in the lists which follow may be assumed to be regular.

☛ IN LEARNING THE IRREGULAR VERBS THE
STUDENT SHOULD MEMORISE THE PRINCIPAL
PARTS: INFINITIVE, PRESENT INDICATIVE, PAST
DEFINITE, FUTURE AND PAST PARTICIPLE. THESE
ESSENTIAL PARTS MUST BE KNOWN, AS FROM
THEM ALL OTHERS CAN BE MADE.

Thus, the way to memorise **POTERE**, *to be able* is:
Potere, posso, potei, potrò, potuto.

¶ *Irregular verbs ending in* **-ARE.**

There are only four irregular verbs in this conjugation: **ANDARE**, *to go* ; **DARE**, *to give* ; **FARE**, *to
make, do* ; **STARE**, *to stand, be, stay.* These four verbs
are of frequent occurrence, and must be known
thoroughly.

ANDARE, *to go.*

Pres. Ind.:	**vado, vai, va, andiamo, andate, vanno.**
Future :	**andrò, andrai, andrà, andremo, andrete, andranno.**
Condit.:	**andrei, andresti, andrebbe, andrem- mo, andreste, andrEbbero.**
Imper.:	**va', vada, andiamo, andate, vAdano.**
Pres. Sub.:	**ch'io vada, che tu vada, ch'egli vada, che andiamo, che andiate, che vA- dano.**

Regular are: the Imperfect, **andavo**, etc.; the Past
Definite, **andai**, etc.; the Imperfect Subjunctive,
ch'io andassi, etc.; the Present Participle, **andante** ;
the Gerund, **andando**[1], and the Past Participle,
andato. The Future and Conditional are sometimes
also conjugated regularly ; as **andrò, andrai;
andrei, andresti,** etc.

[1] The Gerund should be avoided by the beginner—it is given
here merely for reference.

DARE, *to give.*

Pres. Ind.: do, dai, dà, diamo, date, danno.

Past Def.: diedi, desti, diede (dette or diè), demmo, deste, diEdero (dEttero or diErono).

Future: darò, darai, darà, daremo, darete, darAnno.

Condit.: darei, daresti, darebbe, daremmo, dareste darEbbero.

Imp.: dà, día, díamo, date, díano (or díeno).

Pres. Subj.: ch'io, día, che tu día, ch'egli día, che diamo, che diáte, che díano.

Imp. Subj.: ch'io dessi, che tu dessi, ch'egli desse, che dEssimo, che deste, che dEssero.

Regular: Imperfect, dava etc. *Present Participle:* dante, *Gerund:* dando, *Past Participle:* dato.

Ridare, *to give again,* is conjugated in the same way, but takes an accent in the Present Indicative: ridò, ridai, ridà, etc. Derivatives of dare of more than three syllables; as circondare, *to surround,* etc. are conjugated regularly.

FARE, *to make, to do.*

Pres. Ind.: fo (faccio), fai, fa, facciamo, fate, fanno.

Past Def.: feci, facesti, fece, facemmo, faceste, fEcero.

Pres. Sub.: faccia.

Future: farò, etc.

Imp.: fa.

Participles: facente (Pres.); **FATTO** (past). And one of the few useful Gerunds: **FACENDO,** *doing.* Facendo cosí—*doing so,* or *while doing so.*

STARE, to be, to stand, stay.

Pres. Ind.: sto, stai, sta, stiamo, state, stanno.

Past Def.: stetti, stesti, stette, stemmo, steste, stEttero.

Future: starò, starai, starà, staremo, starete, staranno.

Pres. Sub.: stía, stía, stía, stiámo, stiáte, stíano.

Imp.: sta, etc.

Participles: stante, **STATO.**

As already indicated, the four verbs, **andare, dare, fare** and **stare,** are of frequent occurrence and should be known. Another good reason for mastering them completely is that they can be used to form phrases or idioms[1] that are useful. Some of these are given below, but they need not be mastered on a first perusal of this book—let it suffice for the present to know the four verbs well. On second perusal learn the following idioms:—

ANDARE, to go.

Andare a cavallo, to ride.
Andare in carrozza, to drive.
Andare a piedi, to go on foot.
Andare a male, to decay, to decline in health.
Andare di bene in meglio, to get better and better.
Andare di male in peggio, to get worse and worse.
Andare in cóllera, to get angry.
Andare superbo, to be proud.

Andare may be used in the sense of it, he, she, must. **Non va fatto cosí,** It must not be done thus. **Non va svegliato,** He must not be awakened. **Non va lasciata sola,** She must not be left (alone).

FARE, to do, make.

Fare attenzione, to pay attention, be careful.
Far bel tempo—cattivo tempo, to be fine, to be bad weather.
Far caldo—freddo, to be warm, cold (of the weather).
Far colazione, to breakfast.
Far fare, to have done.
Far male, to hurt.

[1] See pages 65 and 91.

Fare il sarto, il calzolaio, *to be a tailor, a shoemaker.*
Fare un bagno—una passeggiata, *to take a bath, a walk.*
Fare un bríndisi, *to drink a toast.*
Fare una visita, *to pay a call, a visit.*
Far le veci di, *to replace, to represent.*
Far naufragio, *to be shipwrecked.*
Far vela, *to set sail.*
Far vista (di), *to pretend.*
Farsi ánimo, *to take courage.*
Farsi beffe (di) *to ridicule, to make fun (of).*

DARE, *to give.*

Dar ad intendere, *to make believe.*
Dar fuoco, *to set on fire.*
Dar del Lei, del voi etc. to address one in the 3rd Person singular—in the 2nd Person Plural (polite and familiar forms).
Dar préstito, *to lend.*
Dar luogo, *to occasion, to give rise to.*
Dar parola, *to give one's word.*
Darsi bel tempo, *to seek one's leisure, ease.*
Darsi pensiero, *to take to heart.*

STARE.

To be well, ill or *badly,* either in health condition or personal appearance is rendered by the verb **Stare** in Italian instead of **Essere.** **Non sta bene,** *He is unwell.* **Sta scOmoda,** *She is uncomfortable.*

Star di casa, *to live, to inhabit.*
Lasciare stare, *to let a person or a thing alone.*
Star allegro or **di buon ánimo,** *to cheer up.*
Star quieto, *to be quiet.*
Star in forse, *to be doubtful.*
Star in piede, *to stand (be on foot).*
Star zitto, *to be silent.*

Verbs which take either the diphthong **uo** when stress is laid on it, or simply the vowel **o** if the tonic accent is on another syllable, may also be considered as irregular verbs, as:—

accorare, *to grieve.*
arrotare, *to sharpen.*
consonare, *to suit.*
giocare, *to play.*
infocare, *to inflame.*
nuotare, *to swim.*

rinnovare, *to renew.*
risonare, *to resound.*
rotare, *to wheel.*
sonare, *to sound, to ring.*
tonare, *to thunder*
votare, *to empty.*

This is a model for these irregular forms:—

Ind. Pres.:	**vuoto, vuoti, vuota, vuOtano.**
Imperat.	**vuota, vuoti, vuOtino.**
Subj. Pres.	**vuoti, vuoti, vuoti, vuOtino.**

An idiom is "some combination of words that is not strictly in accordance with the general structure of the language, and therefore requires a specific explanation or exposition." *Nesfield.* That is one definition. I would say " An idiom is a combination of words which requires a different combination of words to translate it into another language." Thus: " *It IS hot*," becomes in Italian: " *It MAKES hot*," **FA CALDO.**

¶ *IRREGULAR VERBS IN* **-ERE**.

This is the most numerous series of irregular verbs, though many of them are only slightly irregular. For convenience, the **-ERE** verbs may be classified under three heads—

(1) **-ERE** in which the **E** is stressed.
(2) **-ÉRE** in which the **E** is unstressed.
(3) Very irregular **-RE** verbs.

As the second group is the most numerous, and the first the most useful (i.e. of most frequent occurrence) it is worth while to memorise a list of those verbs which have a stressed **-E-**:

AVERE, *to have* (For conjugation see page 44).
CADERE, *to fall.*
DISSUADERE, *to disuade.*
DOLERE, *to pain, ache, grieve.*
DOVERE, *to be obliged, to owe.*
GIACERE, *to lie (down), rest.*
GODERE, *to enjoy.*
PARERE, *to seem, appear.*
PERSUADERE, *to persuade.*
PIACERE, *to please.*
POTERE, *to be able, to be capable of.*

RIMANERE, to remain.
SAPERE, to know.[1]
SEDERE, to sit.
SOLERE, to be wont, accustomed.
TACERE, to be silent.
TEMERE, to fear.
VALERE, to be worth.
VEDERE, to see.
VOLERE, to wish, be willing, want.

Of these only **GODERE** and **TEMERE** are regular (conjugated like **CREDERE**). The others are conjugated as follows:—

¶ *IRREGULAR VERBS ENDING -ERE* (stressed).

CADERE, to fall.

Past Def.: **caddi, cadesti, cadde, cademmo, cadeste, cAddero.**

Future: **cadrò, cadrai, cadrà, cadremo, cadrete, cadranno.**

Condit.: **cadrei, cadresti, cadrebbe, cadremmo, cadreste, cadrEbbero.**

Regular: Present Indicative: **cado,** etc. *Imperfect:* **cadeva** etc. *Imperative:* **cadi,** etc. *Present Subjunctive:* **ch'io cada,** etc. *Past Participle:* **caduto.**

The Future and Conditional are regular.

DISSUADERE, to dissuade.

Past Def.: **dissuasi, dissuadesti, dissuase, dissuademmo, dissuadeste, dissuAsero.**

Past Part.: **dissuaso.**

PersuadEre, to persuade, is conjugated like **dissuadEre.**

[1] **Sapere,** to know (demands intellectual ability).
Conoscere, to know (in a superficial sense) see page 78.

66

DOLERE—more often reflexive—**dolersi,** *to pain, ache, grieve.*

Pres. Ind.: **mi dolgo, ti duoli, si duole, ci doliamo** (or **dolghiamo**) **vi dolete, si dOlgono.**

Past Def.: **mi dolsi, ti dolesti, si dolse, ci dolemmo, vi doleste, si dOlsero.**

Future: **mi dorrò, ti dorrai, si dorrà, ci dorremo, vi dorrete, si dorranno.**

Past Part.: **doluto.**

DOVERE, *to owe, to be obliged, compelled.*

Pres. Ind.: **devo** (or **debbo**), **devi, deve** (**debbe** or **dee**), **dobbiamo, dovete, dEvono** (or **dEbbono**).

Past Def.: **dovei** (or **dovetti**), **dovesti, dovè** (or **dovette**), **dovemmo, doveste, dovErono** (or **dovEttero**).

Future: **dovrò, dovrai, dovrà, dovremo, dovrete, dovranno.**

Pres. Sub.: **ch'io debba, che tu debba, ch'egli debba, che dobbiamo, che dobbiate, che dEbbano.**

Past Part.: **dovuto.**

GIACERE, *to lie down, rest.*

Pres. Ind.: **giaccio, giaci, giace, giacciamo, giacete, giAcciono.**

Past Def.: **giacqui, giacesti, giacque, giacemmo, giaceate, giAcquero.**

Imperative: **giAccia, giAcciano.**

Pres. Subj.: **ch'io giAccia.**

Past Part.: **giaciuto.**

N.B.—**PiacEre,** *to please* and its derivatives are conjugated like **giacEre.**

PARERE, *to appear, seem.*

Pres. Ind.: **paio, pari, pare, paiamo, parete, pAiono.**

Past Def.: **parvi** (or **parsi**), **paresti, parve** (or **parse**), **paremmo, pareste, pArvero** (or **pArsero**).

Past Part.: **parso** (or **paruto**).

Rarely used except in the forms : **mi pare,** *it seems to me;* **mi parve,** *it seemed to me.* Use **SEMBRARE** (reg.) *to seem,* instead.

POTERE, *to be able* (purely physical ability).

Pres. Ind.: **posso, puoi, può, possiamo potete, pOssono.**

Past. Def.: **potei** (or **potetti**), **potesti, potè** (or **potette**), **potemmo, poteste, potErono** (or **potEttero**).

Future: **potrò, potrai, potrà, potremo, potrete, potranno**

Pres. Subj.: **ch'io possa, che tu possa, ch'egli possa che possiamo, che possiate, che pOssano.**

Pres. Part.: **potente:** Gerund: **potendo:** Past Participle: **potuto.** No Imperative.

RIMANERE, *to remain.*

Pres. Ind.: **rimango, rimani, rimane, rimaniamo, rimanete rimAngono.**

Past Def.: **rimasi, rimanesti, rimase, rimanemmo, rimaneste, rimAsero.**

Future: **rimarrò, rimarrai, rimarrà rimarremo, rimarrete, rimarranno.**

Condit.: **rimarrei** etc.

Imp.: **rimanga, rimAngano** (polite forms only).

Pres. Subj.: **ch'io rimanga, che tu rimanga, ch'egli rimanga, che rimaniamo, che rimaniate, che rimAngano.**

Past Part.: **rimasto.**

SAPERE, *to know.*

Pres. Ind.: **so, sai, sa, sappiamo, sapete, sanno.**

Past Def.: **seppi, sapesti, seppe, sapemmo, sapeste, sEppero.**

Future: **saprò, saprai, saprà, sapremo, saprete, saprAnno.**

Condit. **saprei, sapresti, saprebbe, sapremmo, sapreste, saprEbbero.**

Imp.: **sAppia, sAppiano.**

Pres. Subj.: **ch'io sAppia, che tu sAppia, ch'egli, sAppia, che sappiamo, che sappiate, che sAppiano.**

Pres. Part.: **sapiente.**

Past Part.: **saputo.**

Other derivatives of **sapEre** are conjugated in the same way.

SEDERE, *to sit.*

Pres. Ind.: **siedo (or seggo), siedi, siede, sediamo sedete, siEdono.**

Past Def.: **sedei (or sedetti), sedesti, sedè (or sedette), sedemmo, sedeste, sedErono (or sedEttero).**

Future: **sedrò, sedrai, sedrà, sedremo, sedrete, sedranno.**

Condit.: **sedrei, sedresti, sedrebbe, sedremmo, sedreste, sedrEbbero.**

Imp.: **siedi, sieda, siEdano. (segga, sEggano).**

69

F

Pres. Subj. ch'io **sieda,** che tu **sieda,** ch'egli **sieda,** che **sediamo,** che **sediate,** che **siEdano.**

Past Part.: **seduto.**

The shortened regular form of Future and Conditional is also much used: **sedrò** etc.

PossedEre, *to possess* and other derivatives are similarly conjugated:

SedErsi, *to sit down*—also like **sedEre.**

SOLERE, *to be wont.*

Pres. Ind.: **soglio, suoli, suole, sogliamo, solete, sOgliono.**

Imperf.: **solevo, solevi, soleva, solevamo, solevate, solEvano.**

Ger. Pres. **solendo.**

Past Part.: **sOlito.**

The past of this verb has rather the nature of an adjective. Thus: **io sono sOlito** corresponds to its equivalent **io soglio; io ero sOlito** or **io solevo,** etc. meaning *I am, was wont.*

TACERE, *to be silent.*

Pres. Ind.: **taccio, taci, tace, tacciamo, tacete, tAcciono.**

Past Def.: **tacqui, tacesti, tacque, tacemmo, taceste, tacquero.**

Imp.: **taccia, tAcciano.**

Past Part.: **taciuto.**

Avoid confusion with the regular verb **tacciare,** *to accuse.*

TENERE, *to keep, to hold.*

Pres. Ind.: **tengo, tieni, tiene, teniamo, tenete, tEngono.**

70

Past Def.:	tenni, (tenei or tenetti) tenesti, tenne, tenemmo, teneste, tEnnero.
Future:	terrò, terrai, terrà, terremo, terrete, terranno.
Condit.:	terrei, terresti, terrebbe, terremmo, terreste, terrEbbero.
Imp.	tenga, tEngano.
Pres. Subj.:	ch'io tenga, che teniamo.
Past Part.:	tenuto.

Derivatives of tenEre are conjugated in the same way. Compare with **VENIRE**, to come.

VALERE, to be worth.

Pres. Ind.:	valgo, vali, vale, valghiamo (or valiamo), valete, vAlgono (or vAgliono).
Past Def.:	valsi, valesti, valse, valemmo, valeste, vAlsero.
Future:	varrò, varrai, varrà, varremo, varrete, varranno.
Condit.:	varrei, etc.
Pres. Subj.:	ch'io valga.
Past Part.:	valuto or valso (both used).

EquivalEre, to be equivalent; **prevalere**, to prevail, etc. are similarly conjugated.

VEDERE, to see.

Pres. Ind.:	vedo, vedi, vede, vediamo, vedete, vEdono.
Past Def.:	vidi, vedesti, vide, vedemmo, vedeste, vídero.
Future:	vedrò, vedrai, vedrà, vedremo, vedrete, vedranno.
Condit.:	vedrei etc.

Imp.:   **veda, vEdano.**

Pres. Subj.: **ch'io veda.**

Past Part.: **veduto** or **visto** (both in common use).

In the Future and Conditional the full regular form is also used: **vederò,** or **vedrò.**

Other derivatives are conjugated in the same way.

VOLERE, *to wish, to will, want, be willing to.*

Pres. Ind.:   **voglio** (or **vo'**) **vuoi, vuole, vogliamo, volete, vOgliono.**

Past Def.:   **volli, volesti, volle, volemmo, voleste vOllero**

Future: **vorrò, vorrai, vorrà, vorremo, vorrete, vorranno.**

Condit.:   **vorrei,** etc.

Pres. Subj.: **ch'io voglia.**

Past Part.: **voluto.** *Gerund:* **volendo.**

Derivatives are conjugated similarly: **rivolEre,** *to wish again.*

¶ IRREGULAR VERBS ENDING **-ĔRE** (unstressed)[1]

This is the most numerous group in the series of **-ERE** irregular verbs—so numerous that it is worth while learning the short list of essential *regular* un- stressed **-ERE** verbs :—

BATTERE, *to beat*	**PERDERE,** *to lose*
CEDERE, *to yield*	**RICEVERE,** *to receive*
CREDERE, *to believe*	**RIPETERE,** *to repeat*
MESCERE, *to mix*	**SPLENDERE,** *to shine*
PENDERE, *to hang* (from)	**VENDERE,** *to sell*

—all conjugated like **CREDERE,** (see page 41).

[1] Note that the **-Ĕ-** so marked has no such distinguishing (diacritical) sign above it in Italian.

Most of the remaining (unstressed) -ÈRE verbs are irregular only in the Past definite and Past Participle. The Past Definite endings are:

-i, -esti, -e, -emmo, -este, -ero.

The Past Participle is generally irregular, and must be memorized. All other tenses are generally regular.

¶ VERY IRREGULAR VERBS ENDING IN -RE

There are only four verbs ending in -RE which are very irregular, do not come under any of the above heads, and are useful. **ADDURRE** must be known, because all verbs ending in -URRE are similarly conjugated. **BERE** (or **BEVERE**) is an essential verb, and so also is **PORRE**. **TRARRE** must be known, because, like **ADDURRE**, it is the model for many verbs ending -ARRE. So:—

ADDURRE, *to adduce.*
Pres. Part.: **adducente.**
Gerund: **adducendo.**
Past Part.: **addotto.**
Pres. Indic.: **adduco, adduci, adduce, adduciamo, adducete, addUcono.**
Imperf.: **adducevo, adducevi, adduceva, adducevamo, adducevate, adducevano.**
Past Def.: **addussi adducesti, addusse adducEmmo, adduceste, addUssero.**
Future: **addurrò, addurrai, addurrà, addurremo, addurrete, addurranno.**
Imp.: **adduca; addUcano**—Polite forms only.

TRARRE, *to draw.*
Pres. Indic.: **traggo, trai, trae, traiamo, traete, trAggono.**

Imperf.	traeva, traevi, etc.
Past. Def.:	trassi, traesti, trasse, traemmo, traeste, trAssero.
Future:	trarrò, trarrai, etc.
Imp.:	tragga, trAggano (polite forms).
Pres. Subj.:	ch'io tragga, che tu tragga, ch'egli tragga, che traiamo, che traiate, che trAggano.
Imp. Subj.:	ch'io traessi, che tu traessi, etc.
Pres. Part.:	traente.
Gerund:	traendo.
Past Part.:	tratto.

BERE or BEVERE, to drink.[1]

Part.:	bevendo, bevuto.
Pres. Indic.:	bevo, bevi, beve. beviamo, bevete, bEvono.
Imperf.:	bevevo, bevevi, beveva, bevevamo, etc.
Past. Def.:	bevvi (bevetti or bevei) bevesti bevve (bevette), bevemmo, beveste, bEvvero or bevEttero.
Future:	berrò or beverò, berrai or beverai, etc., berremo, etc.
Imp.:	beva, bEvano (Polite forms).

PORRE, to put

Pres. Indic.:	pongo, poni, pone, poniamo, ponete, pOngono.
Imperf.:	ponevo, etc., ponevamo, etc.

[1] This is one of the few verbs of which the alternative form is widely used. In some parts of Italy they say **BEVO**, in others **BEO**, etc.

Past. Def.:	posi, ponesti, pose, ponemmo, etc.
Future:	porrò, etc.
Condit.:	porrei, etc.
Imp.:	poni, ponga, poniamo, ponete, pOngano.
Pres. Subj.:	ponga, poniamo, etc.
Imp. Subj.:	ponessi, etc., ponessimo, etc.

SUPORRE, to suppose, is conjugated similarly.

¶ *IRREGULAR VERBS IN -IRE.*

The essential irregular verbs in **-IRE** are:

DIRE, to say, tell.
MORIRE, to die.
SALIRE, to ascend, mount.
UDIRE, to hear.
USCIRE, to go out, away.
VENIRE, to come.
and their derivatives, which are similarly conjugated.

DIRE, to tell, say.

Pres. Ind.:	dico, dici, dice, diciamo, dite, dícono
Future:	dirò (also dicerò).
Imperf.:	dicevo, etc.
Past. Def.:	dissi, dicesti, disse, dicemmo, diceste, díssero.
Imper.:	di', dica, diciamo, dite, dícano.
Pres. Sub.:	Che io dica, etc.
Gerund:	dicendo.
Past Part.:	DETTO.
Similarly:	contraddire, to contradict. predire, to predict, etc.

75

MORIRE, *to die.*

Pres. Ind.: **muoio, muori, muore, moriamo, morite, muOiono.**

Pres. Sub.: **che io muoia. . . muoia. . . muoia. . moriamo, moriate, muOiano.**

Past Part.: **morto.**

SALIRE, *to ascend.*

Pres. Ind.: **salgo, sali, sale, saliamo, salite, sálgono.**

Pres. Sub.: **che io salga,** etc.

Past Part.: **salito.**

UDIRE, *to hear.*

Pres. Ind.: **odo, odi, ode, udiamo, udite, ódono.**

NOTE. **-u-** changes to **-o-** when the accent falls on the first syllable.

USCIRE, *to go away, out.*

Pres. Ind.: **esco, esci, esce, usciamo, uscite, éscono.**

Past Part.: **uscito.**

Similarly: **riuscire,** *to succeed.*

VENIRE, *to come.*

Pres. Ind.: **vengo, vieni, viene, veniamo, venite, véngono.**

Past Def.: **venni, venisti, venne, venimmo, veniste, vénnero.**

Future: **verrò, verrai,** etc.

Pres. Sub.: **che io venga,** etc.

NOTE.—**avvenire,** *to befall*; **convenire,** *to suit*; **divenire,** *to become*; all similarly conjugated.

Aprire, *to open*; has an irregular past definite **apersi.** Past Part.: **aperto.**
Similarly: **coprire,** *to cover*; **offrire,** *to offer*; **soffrire,** *to suffer*: **copersi, coperto; offersi, offerto; soffersi, sofferto.**

¶ *GENERAL LIST OF USEFUL IRREGULAR VERBS, SOME NOT ALREADY MENTIONED.*

The following list of verbs, irregular only in the Past Definite and Past Participle, is for reference. The student will find that it is not difficult to learn, but he should concentrate first on the words in large type, which are essential:—

Infinitive	Present Indicative	Past Definite	Past Participle
ACCOGLIERE to welcome	accolgo	accolsi	accolto
accórrere to run up, hasten	accorro	accorsi	accorso
accréscere to augment	accresco	accrebbi	accresciuto
affíggere to affix	(like **fíggere**)		
afflíggere to afflict	affliggo	afflissi	afflitto
AGGIUNGERE to add	aggiungo	aggiunsi	aggiunto
AMMETTERE to admit	ammetto	ammisi	ammesso
APPARTENERE to belong	(conjugated like **ténere**)		
APPRENDERE to learn	apprendo	appresi	appreso
APRIRE to open	apro	aprii	aperto

77

árdere	ardo	arsı	arso
to burn			
ASCENDERE	ascendo	ascesi	asceso
to ascend			
ASCONDERE[1]	ascondo	ascosi	ascosto
to hide			
assístere	assisto	assistei	assistito
to assist			
assúmere	assumo	assunsi	assunto
to assume			
atténdere	attendo	attesi	atteso
to wait			
attíngere	attingo	attinsi	attinto
to attain			
cédere	cedo	cessi[2]	cesso
to yield			
CHIEDERE	chiedo	chiesi	chiesto
to ask	(chieggo)	(chiedei chiedetti)	
CHIUDERE	chiudo	chiusi	chiuso
to shut			
cógliere	colgo	colsi	colto
to gather			
COMPRENDERE	comprendo	compresi	compreso
to comprehend			
comprímere	comprimo	compressi	compresso
to compress			
concédere	concedo	concessi	concesso
to concede			
conchiúdere		(like **chiúdere**)	
to conclude			
concórrere		(like **córrere**)	
to concur			
condurre		(like **addurre**)	
to conduct			
conóscere	conosco	conobbi	conosciuto
to know			
contradire		(like **dire**)	
to contradict			
convíncere	convinco	convinsi	convinto
to convince			
coprire	copro	coprii	coperto
to cover			
CORRERE	corro	corsi	corso
to run			

[1] More generally used in the form of **Nascondere**.

[2] More frequently **cedei** or **cedetti**.

78

costruire *to construct*	**costruisco**	**costrussi**[1]	**costrutto**
créscere *to grow*	**cresco**	**crebbi**	**cresciuto**
CUOCERE *to cook*	**cuocio**	**cossi** (**cocei, co-** **cetti**)	**cotto**
decídere *to decide*	**decido**	**decisi**	**deciso**
dedurre *to deduce*		(like **addurre**)	
diféndere *to defend*	**difendo**	**difesi**	**difeso**
dirígere *to direct*	**dirigo**	**diressi**	**diretto**
discéndere *to descend*	**discendo**	**discesi**	**disceso**
dissuadére *to dissuade*	**dissuado**	**dissuasi**	**dissuaso**
distrúggere *to destroy*	**distruggo**	**distrussi**	**distrutto**
DIVIDERE *to divide*	**divido**	**divisi**	**diviso**
eccédere *to exceed*	**eccedo**	**eccedei**	**ecceduto**
eléggere *to elect*	**eleggo**	**elessi**	**eletto**
empìre *to fill*	**empio**	**empii**	**empito**
erígere *to erect*	**erigo**	**eressi**	**eretto**
esclúdere *to exclude*	**escludo**	**esclusi**	**escluso**
ESISTERE *to exist*	**esisto**	**esistei**	**esistito**
esprímere *to express*	**esprimo**	**espressi**	**espresso**
esténdere *to extend*	**estendo**	**estesi**	**esteso**
estínguere *to extinguish*	**estínguo**	**estinsi**	**estinto**
evádere *to evade*	**evado**	**evasi**	**evaso**
fíggere *to fix*	**figgo**	**fissi**	**fitto** (**fisso**)

[1] Also: **costruii**.

79

fíngere to feign	fingo	finsi	finto
frángere to smash	frango	fransi	franto
giúngere to arrive, reach	giungo	giunsi	giunto
(**inclúdere** (**inchiúdere** to include	includo inchiudo	inclusi inchiusi	incluso) inchiuso)
incréscere to increase	incresco	increbbi	incresciuto
insístere to insist	insisto	insistei	insistito
inténdere to understand	intendo	intesi	inteso
intrúdere to intrude	intrudo	intrusi	intruso
invádere to invade	invado	invasi	invaso
LEGGERE to read	leggo	lessi	letto
METTERE to put	metto	misi	messo
MUOVERE to move	muovo	mossi	mosso
NEGLIGERE to neglect	negligo	neglessi	negletto
nuOcere to injure	nuocio	nocqui	nociuto
OCCORRERE to be necessary	(like **córrere**)		
offEndere to offend	offendo	offesi	offeso
OFFRIRE to offer	offro	offrii	offerto
opprímere to oppress	opprimo	oppressi	oppresso
PERDERE to lose	perdo	perdei	perduto
PERMETTERE to permit	permetto	permisi	permesso
persístere to persist	persisto	persistei (persistetti)	persistito

persuadEre *to persuade*	persuado	persuasi	persuaso
piángere *to weep*	piango	piansi	pianto
PIOVERE *to rain*	piove	piovve	piovuto
POSSEDERE *to possess*	possiedo	possedei	posseduto
PRENDERE *to take*	prendo	presi	preso
presúmere *to presume*	presumo	presunsi	presunto
preténdere *to pretend*	pretendo	pretesi	preteso
protéggere *to protect*	proteggo	protessi	protetto
rádere *to shave, erase*	rado	rasi	raso
RENDERE *to give back*	rendo	resi	reso
resistere *to resist*	(like assístere)		
riconóscere *to recognise*	(like conóscere)		
ripréndere *to resume*	(like préndere)		
risólvere *to resolve*	risolvo	risolsi	risolto
RISPONDERE *to respond*	rispondo	risposi	risposto
ROMPERE *to break*	rompo	ruppi	rotto
scégliere *to choose*	scelgo	scelsi	scelto
scéndere *to descend*	scendo	scesi	sceso
scíndere *to separate*	scindo	scissi	scisso
SCOPRIRE *to discover*	scopro	scoprii	scoperto
SCRIVERE *to write*	scrivo	scrissi	scritto
SEDERE *to seat*	siedo	sedei	seduto

81

SOFFRIRE *to suffer*	soffro	soffrii	sofferto
sólvere *to solve*	solvo	solvei	solto
sopprímere *to suppress*	(like opprímere)		
SORPRENDERE *to surprise*	(like préndere)		
spéndere *to spend*	spendo	spesi	speso
TRADURRE *to translate*	(like addure)		
uccídere *to kill*	uccido	uccisi	ucciso
víncere *to vanquish*	vinco	vinsi	vinto
VIVERE *to live**	vivo	vissi	vissuto
vólgere *to turn round*	volgo	volsi	volto

*Future: **Viverò**, or **vivrò**.

ADVERBS

" An adverb is a word used to qualify any part of speech except a noun or pronoun."—*Nesfield.*

Four simple rules enable one to form all the adverbs ever likely to be required, apart from those given on pages 84—6.

Most English adverbs are formed by adding -LY to the adjective. The Italian -**MENTE** (f) meaning *mind*, is used as equivalent ending. Thus, *cold, coldly*: **freddo, freddamente.** Hence:—

RULES TO FORM ADVERBS.

(1) Add -**MENTE** to the *feminine singular* of the adjective: **Freddo, freddamente.**

(2) When the adjective ends -**e**, not preceded by **l** or **r**, simply add -**MENTE**.
Felice, *happy;* **felicemente,** *happily.*

(3) When the adjective ends in **-e** preceded by **l** or **r**, this **-e** is dropped.

Fácile, *easy;* **facilmente,** *easily.*

—and:

(4) Use a preposition with a noun : **con amore,** *lovingly* (with love).

¶ *COMPARISON.*

Comparison follows the same principles as for adjectives (See pages 17—18).

(1)
fácile, *easy.*
caro, *dear.*

(2)
più fácilmente, *easier.*
meno caramente, *less dear.*

(3)
il più fácile, *easiest.*
il meno caro, *least dear.*

The superlative is sometimes formed merely by repeating the positive; **presto,** *soon;* **presto presto** *very soon;* **piano piano,** *very softly.*

¶ *IRREGULAR COMPARISONS.*

bene, meglio, il meglio, *well, better, best.*
male, peggio, il peggio, *badly, worse, worst.*
poco, meno, il meno, *little, less, least.*
molto, più, il più, *very, more, most.*

A few useful adjectives are used as adverbs :

Chiaro, *clear;* **fisso,** *fixed, firm;* **spesso,** *frequent;* **basso,** *deep, base;* **falso,** *false;* **certo,** *certain;* **sicuro,** *sure;* **mezzo,** *half;* **forte,** *strong, loud;* **piano,** *soft, low.*

Thus:

Esso parla chiaro, forte, piano, *He speaks clearly, strongly, softly.*

Now learn the following essential ' invariable ' adverbs.

Note that the list does *not* include adverbs formed from adjectives by adding **-MENTE.**

¶ *LIST OF USEFUL ADVERBS.*

§1. *Affirmation and Negation.*

SÌ, *yes*[1]
infatti, *indeed.*
CERTO
certamente } *surely certainly.*
sicuramente
DAVVERO, *truly, really.*
SENZA DUBBIO, *un-doubtedly.*
NO, *no.*
NON, *not.*
NÈ—NÈ, *neither—nor.*
veramente, *truly.*
NON—CHE, *only.*
NON—MAI, *never.*

NON—PUNTO, *not at all.*
non—già, *not—even.*
NON—PIÙ, *not—any more, no longer.*
neanche
NEPPURE } *not even.*
GIÀ, *already, just now.*
appunto, *exactly (just) so.*
non—mica, *not—certainly.*
NON—ANCORA, *not —yet.*
in nessun modo, *by no means.*

§2. *Choice and Doubt.*

SOPRATTUTTO, *esp-ecially.*
FINALMENTE, *finally.*
PERCHÈ? *why?*
PERCHÈ, *because.*
perciò, *that is why, how-ever.*

FORSE, *perhaps.*
CIRCA, *about.*
PROBABILMENTE, *probably.*
PIUTTOSTO, *rather.*
prima di tutto, *first of all.*

[1] Essential Adverbs are in large type.

§3. Adverbs of Place.

DOVE, *where, whither.*
onde, donde, *where from, whence.*
QUI }*here, hither, this*
qua }*way.*
LÀ, LÌ,[1] *there, thither.*
VI, CI (French y), *here, there.*
SOPRA }*on, upon.*
SU }
DI SOPRA, *above, upstairs.*
DI SOTTO, *below, downstairs.*
da parte, *aside.*
lassù, *up there.*
GIÙ, *below, down.*
laggiù, *down there.*
quassù, *up here.*
quaggiù, *down here.*
in su, *upwards.*
in giù, *downwards.*
abbasso, *down.*

DENTRO, *within.*
DIETRO, *behind.*
indietro, *behind, backwards.*
SOTTO, *below.*
A DESTRA, a diritta, *on the right.*
A SINISTRA, a manca, *on the left.*
innanzi, *before, forward.*
davanti, *before, forward.*
AVANTI, *forward, along.*
dentro, entro, *therein, within.*
FUORI, *outside, out.*
da per tutto }
dappertutto }*everywhere.*
ognidove }
qualche luogo, *somewhere.*
altronde }*elsewhere.*
altrove }
ovunque, *wherever.*

§4. Adverbs of Quantity.

MOLTO, *much, very* (much).
assai, *much* (enough).
TROPPO, *too, too much.*
TANTO, *so, so much.*
ABBASTANZA, *enough.*
di più (any) *more.*
eziandio, *also, even, yet.*

PURE }*even, even*
pur anco }*yet.*
SOLAMENTE, *only.*
SOLTANTO, SOLO, *only.*
nonchè, *also.*
POCO, *little.*
PIÙ, di più, *more.*

[1] N.B.: **Qui** (here) near the speaker; **Lì,** near the person spoken to; and **Là,** away from them both.

MENO, *less.*
QUANTO? *how much?*
TANTO—QUANTO,
  so much—as.

tanto più (meno), *so much the more (less).*

§5. *Miscellaneous Adverbial Expressions.*

a mente ⎫ *by heart.*
a memoria ⎭
in fretta, *in haste, hastily.*
in furia, *in a hurry.*
invano, *in vain.*
con cómodo, *leisurely.*
a stento, *hardly, with difficulty.*
di frequente, *frequently.*
di sólito, *generally, usually.*
APPENA, *scarcely.*
a buon mercato, *cheaply.*
a voce, *aloud.*
apposta, *on purpose.*
a caso, *by accident, chance.*

ad alta voce, *aloud.*
ADESSO, *now.*
adesso adesso, *by and by.*
fra breve, *shortly.*
a poco a poco, *little by little.*
in breve, *shortly.*
per lo più, *mostly.*
a proposito, *quite conveniently, by the by.*
per bocca, *verbally, by word of mouth.*
tutt'al più, *at the most.*
dapprima, *first.*
APPUNTO, *exactly.*

PREPOSITIONS

" A preposition is a word placed before a noun to show in what relation the person or thing denoted thereby stands to something else." *Nesfield.*

(For prepositions which form contractions with the article see page 10).

a, *at.*
con, *with.*
di, *of.*
da, *of, from, by.*
avanti, *before.*
contro, *against.*
erso, *towards.*

dopo, *after.*
durante, *during.*
fra ⎫ *between.*
tra ⎭
lungo, *along.*
giusta, *according to.*
in, *in, within.*

lungo, *along.*
per, *for, by.*
secondo, *according to.*
malgrado, *notwithstand-ing.*
mediante, *by means of.*
oltre, *besides, beyond.*

eccetto ⎫ *except.*
salvo ⎭
senza, *without.*
sopra, *on, upon, over.*
sotto, *under.*
su (sur, in su) *over, upon.*

All other prepositions may be followed by **DI, A** or **DA.**

PREPOSITIONS GENERALLY FOLLOWED BY DI.

Fuori (di), *out (of) outside.*
al di là, *on the other side.*
al di quà, *on this side.*
al di sopra, *above.*
presso, *near.*
a torza dl, *by dint of.*
prima, *(of time) before.*
di sotto, *underneath.*
di dentro, *within.*
di fuori, *outside.*
a seconda di, *according to.*
a modo, *in the manner.*

alla volta di, *in the direction of.*
a causa, *by reason of.*
a ragione, *on account of.*
per mezzo, *by means.*
in luogo ⎫ *instead.*
invece ⎭
a ple, *at the foot.*
a dispetto, *in spite of.*
in favore, *in favour.*

PREPOSITIONS GENERALLY FOLLOWED BY A.

Fino, *till, as far as.*
in faccia, *opposite.*
circa ⎫ *about.*
incirca ⎭
in mezzo, *amidst.*
dentro, *inside.*
innanzi ⎫
dinanzi ⎬ *before.*
davanti ⎭
attorno, *around, all round.*

in rispetto ⎫ *concerning.*
inquanto ⎭
dietro, ⎫ *behind.*
di dietro, ⎭
accanto, *beside.*
intorno, *about.*
vicino, *near.*
conforme, *as.*
rincontro, *against, opposite.*

PREPOSITIONS GENERALLY FOLLOWED BY DA

lontano ⎫ *far.*
lungi ⎭
fin da, *from.*
infuori, *except.*

There are few reliable rules for the subtle usage of pre-positions and the student is advised for a beginning to be satisfied with knowing the simple equivalents given above.

He should, however, note carefully that **DA** is the preposition of *agency, cause, fitness* and *source*, thus:

Il ragazzo fu punito dal maestro, *The boy was punished BY the master.*

Essa fu soffocata dal fumo, *She was suffocated BY the smoke.*

Discende da poveri cittadini, *He is descended FROM poor citizens.*

Un uomo dabbene, *An honest man.*

Un uomo da poco, *A good-for-nothing man.*

Tira a suo padre, *He takes after his father.*

Egli combattè da eroe, *He fought like a hero.*

Lo trattò da prìncipe, *He treated him like a prince.*

È una cosa da sorprendere, da ridere, da deplorare, *It is a surprising, laughable, deplorable thing.*

Egli dà da lavorare, da mangiare, *He gives work, the wherewithal to eat.*

Non è acqua da bere, *It is not water fit to drink.*

Vi parlo da amico, *I speak to you as a friend.*

Ho da dírvelo, *I have to tell you.*

Un calzolaio da donna, *A ladies' shoemaker.*

La bella dagli occhi azzurri, *The blue-eyed beauty.*

Un letto da monarca, *A bed for a monarch.*

The preposition **di** is used for the English prepositon *to* when prefixed to an infinitive preceded by another verb, as: *I promise you to come,* **Vi prometto di venire.** *He has told him not to speak,* **Gli ha detto di non parlare.** *He was not afraid to say it,* **Non aveva paura di dirlo.** But, should the first verb imply motion, the preposition to is translated by **a** as: *I am going to see Edward,* **Vado a vedere Edoardo.** *He has been to pay him a visit,* **È stato a fargli visita.**

The verbs **potere, sapere, dovere, volere, fare, lasciare, bisognare, bastare,** and **convenire** do not require a preposition before an infinitive which follows them:

Non potrò venire, *I shall not be able to come.*

CONJUNCTIONS

Conjunctions are words used for connecting words or sentences. For example: "You *and* I," "My brother *and* I are good friends, *but* he is much older than I."
And and *but* are the conjunctions.

In the following list, the words in large type are essentials :—

SE, if.
E PURE } and yet.[1]
EPPURE }
tanto-quanto, as well as.
QUANDO, when.
COME, as.
finchè, as long as.
DOPO CHE, after.
APPENA } scarcely.
a pena }
SUPPOSTO CHE, supposing, provided that.
ANCHE, also.
allorchè, then, when.
PERCHÈ }
poichè } because,
giacchè } since, as.
siccome }
posciachè, after that, since.
O, or (od before a vowel).
O—O, either—or.
ovvero } or.
oppure }
benchè } though,
sebbene } although.
ancorchè }
però } however, yet.
pertanto }
NÈ—NÈ, neither—nor.

ora—ora, now—now.
CHE, that.
E and (**ed** before a word beginning with a vowel).
sicchè, so that.
AFFINCHÈ, so that, in order to.
PRIMA CHE, before, sooner.
quand'anche, though, although.
se anche, even if.
di maniera che } so that.
di modo che }
tosto che } as soon as, at
súbito che } the time.
PERÒ, though, however, therefore.
DUNQUE, so, therefore.
quindi, therefore, consequently.
dacchè, because, since.
MENTRE, whilst, etc.
fin a tanto che, as long as.
ANZI, on the contrary, even.
NEPPURE, not even.
SENZA CHE, without.
MA ANCHE, but also.

[1] The student will notice that, in the lists of adverbs, prepositions and conjunctions, he will find words repeated. The distinction between a word used as an adverb, preposition and conjunction is a grammatical subtlety. If the *word* is known, that is sufficient for the present.

non ostante che, *notwithstanding.*

per quanto, *however.*

non perciò, *nevertheless.*

nullameno } *nevertheless*
nientemeno }

per altro, *however.*

MA, *but.*

—and the following[1] which must always be used with the subjunctive:—

Affinchè, *in order that*

a meno che, *unless*

a patto che, *on condition that*

benchè, *although*

comecchè, *as if*

dato che, *given that.*

nel caso che, *in case that*

nonostante che, *notwithstanding that*

posto che, *granted that*

prima che, *before*

purchè, *provided that*

qualora, *if*

quandanche, *even if*

quandochè, *even when*

sebbene, *though*

semprechè, *always granted that.* (See page 58).

INTERJECTIONS

Interjections are words used to express a feeling or emotion, as for example:—

joy, **bene! bravo! viva!**

sorrow, **ahi! ohi! ahimè! ohimè!**

silence, **zitto!**

wish, **magari!**

doubt, **mah!**

disdain, **oibò!**

surprise, **oh!**

fear, **uh! guai!**

Also:—

Ecco, *here is, here are,* may be joined to a pronoun: **éccomi,** *here I am;* **éccoli,** *here they are;* **éccone,** *here is some of it.* (See page 26).

NOTE.—**ADD/O!** *adieu!* **ARRIVEDERCI!** *good-bye!* **ben arrivato!** *welcome!*

[1] See page 57.

IDIOMS

For definition of an idiom, see footnote on page 65. Italian is rich in idioms, and they are the part of the language which must be learnt by experience rather than from books. But here are some elementary and essential idioms which must be known:—

Aver appetito, *to be hungry.*
Aver ragione, *to be right.*
Chiamarsi, *to be called, named.*
Aver caldo, *to be hot.*
Mi piace—, *I like—.*
Non mi piace—, *I do not like—.*
Davvero? *Really?*
Da quanto tempo? *How long since?*
Sono nato il—, *I was born on—.*
Quante volte? *How often?*
Di nuovo, *again.*
Aver fretta, *to be in a hurry.*
Aver sete, *to be thirsty.*
Aver torto, *to be wrong.*
Come si chiama lei? *What is your name?*
Aver freddo, *to be cold.*
Niente affatto, *not at all.*
A me pure, *I also, to me also.*
Nemmeno io, lui; *Nor I, he, etc.*
Che c'è di nuovo? *What news?*
Lo faccia di nuovo, *Do it again!*
Di più, *most, the best.*
Questo è che mi piace di più. *That is what pleases me best, most.*
Come sta lei? *How are you?*

Lungo, largo and **alto,** are used for *length, breadth* and *height:* **Questa stanza è lunga 10 piedi, larga 20 ed alta 8.** *This room is 10 feet long, 20 broad (or wide) and 8 high.*

Other idioms will be found on pages 63–65.

CORRESPONDENCE

The date is written thus: **3 Gennaio 1937; 2 Marzo 1938,** etc., but the first of a month is always **1°** (representing **primo,** the ordinal number).

In Italian commercial correspondence the opening salutation (Dear Sir, Madam, etc.) is generally omitted, and this applies to most formal correspondence. When the correspondence is informal, or purely private, then Dear Sir, Madam etc. may be expressed as follows:

(*a*) when the name of the person addressed is added

Egregio Signor Colaluca } *Dear Mr. Colaluca.*
Pregiato Signor Colaluca

(*b*) when the name of the person addressed is omitted:

Egregio Signore } *Dear Sir.*
Pregiato Signore

—or one may say **Stimato Signor Colaluca, Stimato Signore**—.

To a lady one writes:
Gentilíssima Signora, or
Gentilíssima Signorina.
—adding her name, if on terms of friendship.

A very familiar opening is: **Caro mio,** or **Cara mia;** or, **Mio caro amico, Cara amica mia.** The beginner should be careful about using these openings.

ENDINGS: The endings for letters in Italian are elaborate, and the student is advised to keep to the following:—

Familiar: **DevotIssimo suo,**—*Yours very sincerely.*
Formal: **Colla mAssima stima, vi saluto,**—
         Yours faithfully.

NOTE.—In commercial correspondence, the Second Person Plural is used, and, as the opening and ending formulae are somewhat elaborate, the student must refer to one of the many books dealing with this special aspect of the subject.

In addressing an envelope write:

Egregio Sig. Colaluca, or
Gentilísima Signora Colaluca.

c/o is expressed by the word **Presso.**

Part II.
THE ESSENTIAL VOCABULARY

NOTE ON THE
ESSENTIAL VOCABULARY OF ITALIAN

In order to express more than 90 per cent. of the ideas of everyday life, a vocabulary of about 1150 words is necessary in Italian. The student must master the pronouns, the numbers; certain adverbs, prepositions, conjunctions and interjections given from page 84 to page 90 ; the names of the days of the week, the months of the year, a few common idioms and the proper names, and the vocabulary in the alphabetical list on pages 99–131. This represents the essential vocabulary of the language which, used in accordance with grammar, provides the student with a working vocabulary of several thousand words, and will enable him or her to pick up the average Italian newspaper or book, confident that most of it can be understood.

It has been ascertained that a beginner can memorize 20-30 new words of a foreign language in an hour ; after a few hour's practice the number increases. The Essential Vocabulary of Italian, and the general principles of the grammar, can be assimilated in a couple of months. Those students who know Latin or one of the Romance languages, will learn more rapidly than those who do not. All will find that Italian contains a large number of words which greatly resemble their English equivalents, and are assimilated with little effort.

☛ Know the vocabulary BOTH WAYS: **L'uomo,** *the man; the man,* **L'uomo**. Speak words aloud when memorizing them. Thus, from the very beginning of the learning process repeat the word with its equivalent bath ways until it is recognizable both ways, and by *sight* and by *sound*. Repetition should be continued until meaning and pronunciation come without hesitation. AS EACH WORD IS BEING MEMORIZED AN IMAGE OF THE THING OR AN ASSOCIATION OF THE IDEA SHOULD BE IN THE MIND. This not only facilitates learning by making it more interesting, but it accustoms the learner *to think* in Italian. So, when learning the Italian word **città,** *city,* think of the city with which you are most familiar, its streets, houses, people and traffic. The more the imagination is used to assist memory in this way, the more rapid will be the progress in the language.

See statistical note on page 144.

THE ESSENTIAL VOCABULARY

¶ *DAYS OF THE WEEK, MONTHS, SEASONS AND PROPER NAMES.*

§1. *Days of the Week.*

Lunedì, *Monday.*	**Giovedì,** *Thursday.*
Martedì, *Tuesday.*	**Venerdì,** *Friday.*
Mercoledì, *Wednesday.*	**SAbato,** *Saturday.*

DomEnica, *Sunday.*

(All masculine except the last).

§2. *Months of the Year.*

Gennaio, Febbraio, Marzo, Aprile, Maggio, Giugno, Luglio, Agosto, Settembre, Ottobre, Novembre, Dicembre.

§3. *Seasons.*

La primavera, *spring.*	**L'autunno,** *autumn.*
L'estate (masc.), *summer.*	**L'inverno,** *winter.*

La stagione, *the season.*

97

§4. Points of the Compass.

Nord, *North.*   **Est,** *East.*
Sud, *South.*   **Ovest,** *West.*

§5. Proper Names and Adjectives.

L'Europa, *Europe.*
L'Italia, *Italy.*
L'Inghilterra, *England.*
La Francia, *France.*
La Germania, *Germany.*
La Svizzera, *Switzerland.*
La Spagna, *Spain.*
Il Portogallo, *Portugal.*
La Russia, *Russia.*
Gli Stati Uniti, the *U.S.(A.).*
La Gran Brettagna, *Great Britain.*

europEo, *European* (**-a,** *-woman*).
italiano, *Italian.*
inglese, *Englishman.*
francese, *Frenchman.*
tedesco, *German.*
svIzzero, *Swiss.*
spagnOlo, *Spanish.*
portoghese, *Portuguese.*
russo, *Russian.*
americano, *American.*

Londra, *London;* **Parigi,** *Paris;* **Berlino,** *Berlin;* **Roma,** *Rome;* **Torino,** *Turin;* **NApoli,** *Naples;* **GEnova,** *Genoa;* **Firenze,** *Florence;* **VenEzia,** *Venice;* **Milano,** *Milan;* **Livorno,** *Leghorn;* **Le Alpi,** *The Alps;* **La MAnica,** *The English Channel;* **Il MediterrAneo,** *The Mediterranean.*

ALPHABETICAL LIST OF ITALIAN WORDS.

See note on The Essential Vocabulary of Italian on page 96.

The following alphabetical list is for repetition and reference. Words in BOLD CAPITALS should be learnt first as they are essential; the remainder may be approached later. Stress is indicated either by an accent or by printing the stressed letter in a distinctive type.

A

ABBASTANZA, enough.

abbisognare, to be necessary.

abbondare, to abound (in).

abbreviare, to abridge, shorten.

ABILE, clever, skilful.

ABILITÀ, ability, skill.

ABITO, dress, clothes, costume, habit.

ABITUARSI, to accustom one's self.

abominare, to hate, abominate.

accadEmia, academy.

ACCADERE, to happen.

accEndere, to set on fire, light.

accento, accent.

ACCETTARE, to accept.

ACCIAIO, steel.

ACCIDENTE, (m.) accident, chance, misfortune.

ACCÓGLIERE, together, welcome, receive with good will.

accomodare, to accommodate.

ACCOMODARSI, to sit down, be at ease.

ACCOMPAGNARE, to accompany.

accordare, to accord, grant.

¹ D'accordo! Agreed!

accordarsi, to agree (with).

ACCORDO¹, accord, agreement (harmony).

accorgErsi, to notice (with shrewdness).

ACCOSTUMARE, to accustom.

ACCOSTUMARSI, to be used to.

accumulare, to accumulate, heap up.

ACCURATO, accurate.

accusare, to accuse.

ACQUA, water.

ADAGIO, slowly, softly.

ADDIO, adieu, farewell.

ADDIZIONE, addition (bill).

addormentarsi, to fall asleep.

adoperare, to employ (in work).

AEREO, aerial.

affannare, to grieve (about)

affanno, grief, anxiety.

affare, affair, business.

affermare, to affirm, assert.

affezionarsi, to become attached to, to like.

affezionato, fond, affectionate.

99

AFFISSO, fixed, attached to.

AFFRETTARSI, to hurry.

AGENTE, agent.

aggiUngere, to join to, add, reach.

aggiunto, added, attached to.

aggiustare, to adjust.

AGGRADEVOLE, agreeable, pleasant.

agiato, at ease, rich.

AGIO, ease, comfort.

AGUZZO, sharp, edged.

AIUTANTE, assistant.

AIUTARE, to assist, help.

AIUTO, assistance.

ALA, wing.

albergo, hotel, inn.

albero, tree.

álcool, alcohol

ALIENO, alien, foreign.

ALIMENTO, nourishment, food.

allarme (m), alarm.

allegrIa, happiness.

ALLEGRO, gay, cheerful.

altezza, height.

ALTO, high.

alzare, to lift, raise.

alzarsi, to get up, rise.

amAbile, lovable.

AMARE, to love, be fond of.

amarezza, bitterness.

AMARO, bitter.

ameno, pleasing, charming.

AMICO, friend.

AMISTÀ, friendship.

AMMALATO, sick.

ammazzare, to kill, murder.

ammEttere, to admit, grant.

amministrare, to administer.

ammirare, to admire, envy.

AMORE (m.), love.

ANDARE, to go, walk.

andArsene, to go away, to get out of.

anello, ring.

ANGOLO, angle, corner

angusto, narrow.

Anima, soul, spirit.

ANIMALE, animal.

ANIMO, mind, intelligence.

annesso, annexed.

ANNO, year.

annoiArsi, to get annoyed.

annuale, annual.

annunziare, to announce.

ansietà, anxiety.

ansioso, anxious, eager.

antichità, antiquity.

antico, antique, old.

antipAtico, disagreeable.

anziano, ancient.

100

APERTA, hole, opening.

APERTO, open, evident.

apparato

APPARECCHIO apparatus, what is seen, show, preparation.

APPARTENERE, to belong to, to concern.

APPETITO, appetite.

applaudire, to applaud.

applauso, applause.

applicare, to apply.

applicarsi, to apply, devote one's self to.

appoggiare, to lean —si (against).

apprEndere, to learn (also to teach).

appuntare, to point, sharpen.

APPUNTO, precise (-ly)

APRIRE, to open.

arancio, orange.

arbitrare, to arbitrate.

architetto, architect.

arco, bow, arch.

arcuato, arched, curved.

ARENA, sand.

ARGENTO, silver.

ARIA, air.

Arido, arid, dry.

aritmEtica, arithmetic.

ARME (f.), weapon, arms.

ARRIVARE, to arrive.

ARRIVO, arrival

arrostire, to roast.

ARTE (f), art, skill.

artIcolo, article.

artista, artist.

ascEndere, to ascend, mount, go up.

ASCOLTARE, to listen (to).

Asino, ass, donkey.

ASPETTARE, to expect, hope for.

assalto, assault.

asse (m.), axis.

assegno, assignment, order.

assemblEa, assembly.

ASSENTARSI, to absent one's self.

assente, absent.

assenza, absence.

assicurare, to assure.

ASSISTERE, to be present.

assiso, sitting, seated

assoluto, absolute.

assunto, undertaking.

assurdo, absurd.

astro, star, heavenly body.

astuto, astute, crafty.

atmosfera, atmosphere

attento, attentive

ATTENZIONE, attention.

attirare, to attract, draw to.

ATTIVITÀ, activity.

attivo, active, lively.

ATTO, act, action.

attOnito, astonished.

attore[1], *actor.*

ATTRATTIVO, *attractive.*

ATTRAVERSARE, to *cross, traverse.*

ATTUALE, *actual, real, present.*

AUDACE, *audacious, brave.*

AUMENTARE, to *increase, augment.*

ausilio, *help.*

austero, *austere, stern.*

automObile (f), *automobile.*

autore, *author.*

AUTORITÀ, *authority.*

AVANTI, *before, sooner, (forward!)*

AVANZARE, to *advance.*

avaro, *avaricious, greedy.*

AVERE, to *have.*

Avido, *avid, greedy.*

avo, *grandfather.*

avvantaggio, *avantage.*

avventurarsi, to *risk.*

AVVERTIRE, to *warn, advise of.*

avvisare, to *inform.*

AVVISO, *advice, notice.*

avvocare, to *plead.*

avvocato, *advocate, lawyer.*

AZIONE, *action, deed.*

azzurro, *azure, light blue.*

B

baciare, to *kiss.*

bAcio, *kiss.*

bagaglio, *baggage.*

bagnarsi, to *bathe, take a bath.*

BAGNO, *bath.*

baia, *joke.*

balbutire, to *stammer.*

BALENO, *lightning.*

ballo, *ball, dance.*

balza, *rock, cliff.*

bambino, *baby.*

BANCA, *bank.*

banchiEre, *banker.*

BANCO, *bench, seat.*

banda, *band, troop.*

bandiera, *banner.*

BARBA, *beard.*

barbiere, *barber*

barbuto, *bearded.*

BASE (f.), *base, basis.*

BASSO, *low, mean, base.*

BASTA, *enough.*

bastante, *sufficient.*

bastone (m.), *staff, truncheon, stick.*

battaglia, *battle.*

BATTERE, to *beat.*

baule (m.), *trunk, box.*

beato, *blessed.*

BELLEZZA, *beauty.*

bellicoso, *martial, warlike.*

---

[1] Fem. **attrice**, *actress.*

BELLO, beautiful, handsome.

BENAVVENTURATO lucky.

benedetto, blessed.

benefattore, benefactor.

beneficio } benefit,

BENEFIZIO } kindness.

berretta, cap.

bestia, beast.

BEVÉRE (or bere), to drink.

BIANCO, white.

biblioteca, library.

bicchiere (m.), beaker, glass.

bigio, grey.

biglietto, ticket.

bilancia, balance, scale.

biondo, blond, fair.

birra, beer.

bisavo, great-grandfather.

bisbiglio, whisper.

biscotto, biscuit.

bisogna, business, affair.

BISOGNARE, to be necessary.

BISOGNO, want, need.

bisognoso, needy.

bistorto, crooked, deceitful

BIZZARRO, odd, fantastic.

blando, bland, soft.

BOCCA, month. mouth.

bollire, to boil.

bollo, seal, stamp.

bordo, border.

borgo, borough.

BORSA, purse, exchange.

BOSCO, wood, forest.

BOTTEGA, shop.

BOTTIGLIA, bottle.

BRACCIO, arm.

bravare, to defy.

BRAVO, able, skilful.

bravura, skilfulness.

breccia, breach.

BREVE, brief(-ly).

brevità, brevity.

brigata, brigade.

brillante, brilliant.

brillare, to glitter.

brindisi, toast, health.

BRIO, vivacity.

bronzo, bronze.

bruciare, to burn (int.),

BRUNO, brown.

brusco, rough.

BRUTO, brute.

BRUTTO, ugly.

BUCA, hole, hollow.

bUe[1] (m.) (also bOve), ox.

BUGIA, lie, falsehood.

bugiardo, liar.

BUONO, good, kind.

BURLA, trick.

BURLARE, to jest.

burlesco, burlesque.

burrasca, tempest, storm.

BURRO, butter.

[1] Note: **carne di bue,** beef.

103

C

cacciare, to hunt, chase.

cacciatore, hunter.

cadenza, fall, cadence.

CADERE, to fall.

caduco, frail.

caduta, fall (n.f.).

CAFFÈ, coffee, coffee-house.

CAGIONE (f.), cause, reason.

calamità, calamity.

calca, dense, crowd.

calce (f.), chalk, lime.

CALCOLARE, to calculate.

cAlcolo, calculation.

CALDO, hot.

calendario, calendar.

CALORE (m.), heat.

calvo, bald.

calza, stocking.

calzoni (plur.), trousers.

CAMBIARE, to change.

CAMBIO, change, exchange.

CAMERA, chamber, room.

cameriere, waiter.

cameriera, maid, waitress.

camicia, shirt.

CAMMINARE, to travel, walk.

CAMMINO, way, journey, road.

CAMPAGNA, country.

campagnolo, countryman.

CAMPO, field.

canaglia, rabble.

canale (m.), canal.

CANE, dog.

CANTARE, to sing.

cantatore, singer.

CANTO, (1) song, singing, (2) side, corner.

CAPACE, capable.

capacità, capacity.

capello, single hair.

CAPELLI, hair (of the head.)

CAPIRE, to understand. (also means capable of containing.)

CAPITALE, capital.

capitano, captain.

capItolo, chapter.

CAPO,[1] head, beginning, chief, leader.

capolavoro, masterpiece.

cappello, hat.

CARATTERE, character, dispositon.

CARBONE (m.), coal.

cArcere (m.), prison.

carestía, dearth, famine.

cArica, charge, load.

caricare, to charge, to load.

carità, charity.

CARNE (f.), flesh, meat.

[1]Capo makes many compounds and phrases: Capo d'anno, New Year's Day; capostazione, stationmaster, etc. Look up a good dictionary.

CARO, dear, beloved.

CARRO, car.

carrozza, coach.

CARTA, paper, card

CASA, house, family.

caserma, barrack.

CASO, case, chance, event.

CASSA, chest, money-box.

castello, castle.

casto, chaste.

CATENA, chain.

cattedrale, cathedral.

CATTIVO, wicked, bad.

CAUSA, cause.

causare, to cause.

cautela, caution, bail.

cavaliere,[1] knight, horse-man.

CAVALLO, horse.

cavità, cavity.

CAVO, hollow.

cecità, blindness.

CELEBRE, famous.

cena, supper.

cEncio, rag.

cEnere (fem.), ashes, cinders.

cenno, sign.

censura, censure.

centEsimo, hundredth part.

centro, centre.

centuria, century, company of 100.

cera, wax, wax-candle.

CERCARE, to seek.

cErchio, circle.

certezza, certainty.

CERTO, certain, -ly

cervello, brains.

cesta, basket.

cheto, quiet.

CHIAMARE, to call.

chiarezza, clearness.

CHIARO, clear, bright.

CHIAVE (f.), key.

CHIEDERE, to demand.

chiesa, church.

chiesta, demand, request.

CHIMICA, chemistry.

chímico, chemist (also adj. chemical).

chinare, to bend, incline.

chino, bent, stooped.

chiodo, nail.

chirurgo, surgeon.

chiUdere, to close, en-close.

CHIUSO, closed, shut.

cibare, to feed. (trans.)

CIBO, food, nourishment.

cicatrice (fem.), scar.

CIECO, blind.

CIELO, heaven, sky.

cifra, cipher.

cilindro, cylinder.

CIMA, summit.

cimitero, cemetery.

CIRCOLO, circle, ring.

CIRCOSTANZA, circumstance.

[1] **Cavaliere** is also a title.

citare, to cite.

CITTÀ, city, town.

cittadino, citizen.

civile, civil (of a city).

classe (fem.), class.

cliente, client.

CLIMA (masc.), climate.

coda, tail.

CÓGLIERE, to gather.

cognato, kindred, brother-in-law.

collegio, college.

cOllera, anger.

COLLEZIONE, collection.

collina, hill.

collo, neck, summit.

colonia, colony.

colonna, column.

COLORE (m.), colour.

COLPA, fault.

COLPO, blow, stroke.

COLTELLO, knife, table knife.

COLTO, cultivated, cultured.

COMBATTERE, to fight.

combinazione, combination.

CÓMICO, comical.

COMINCIARE, to begin.

COMMEDIA, comedy.

COMMERCIANTE, merchant.

COMMERCIO, trade.

CÓMODO, convenient.

COMPAGNIA, company.

composizione, composition.

compra, purchase.

COMPRARE, to buy.

comprEndere, to comprehend, understand.

comUne, common, ordinary.

concerto, concert, agreement.

condizione, condition.

condotta, conduct.

condUrre, to conduct.

confessare, to confess.

CONFIDARE, to trust.

CONFIDENZA, confidence.

CONFORME, conformable, conformably.

CONFUSO, confused.

congresso, congress.

connEttere, to connect, join.

CONOSCENZA, acquaintance, knowledge.

CONÓSCERE, to know.

CONOSCIUTO, known.

CONQUISTA, conquest

CONQUISTARE, to conquer.

CONSEGUENTE, following.

CONSEGUENZA, consequence.

CONSEGUIRE, to obtain.

consentire, to consent.

considerare, to consider.

consigliare, to advise.

CONSIGLIO, counsel, advice.

consístere, to consist.

consultare, to consult.

consumare, to consume.

contante (danaro), ready money.

CONTARE, to count.

CONTATTO, contact.

CONTENTO, content.

CONTENUTO, contained.

CONTINUARE, to continue.

CONTINUO, continuous.

CONTO, account, story.

contraddire, to contradict.

CONTRARIO, contrary.

contrasto, contrast.

contrattempo, misfortune

controllo, control.

contratto, contract.

CONVERSAZIONE, conversation.

convito, banquet.

COPIA, copy.

coppia, couple.

CORAGGIO, courage.

corda, cord.

coro, chorus, choir.

corona, crown.

CORPO, body.

corrente, current.

CORSO, course.

corte (f.), court, court-yard.

cortina, curtain.

CORTO, short.

COSA, thing.

COSTARE, to cost.

costume (m.), custom.

credenza, belief.

CREDERE, to believe.

CREDITO, credit.

crema, cream.

crEscere, to grow.

crisi (fem.), crisis.

criticare, to criticise.

CROCE, cross.

crudEle, cruel.

crudeltà, cruelty.

crudo, raw.

CUCCHIAIO, spoon.

cucina, kitchen.

cucire, to sew, stitch.

cugino, cousin.

CUOCĚRE, to cook, boil.

CUORE (m.), heart.

cura, care, cure, parish.

CURIOSO, curious.

D

DANARO, money.

danno, damage.

dannoso, hurtful.

danzare, to dance.

DARE, to give.

DATA, date.

DAVVERO, in truth.

DEBITO, due, debt, debit.

DEBOLE, feeble, faint.

decreto, decree.

defunto, deceased.

degnare, to condescend.

degno, worthy.

delicatezza, delicacy.

DELICATO, delicate.

delitto, crime.

delizia, delight.

delizioso, delicious.

demenza, madness.

DENTE (m.), tooth.

DESTINO, destiny.

DESTRA, right (hand).

A DESTRA, to the right.

destro, dextrous.

dialetto, dialect.

diario, diary.

diAvolo, devil.

difEndĕre, to defend.

difesa, defence.

difetto, defect.

DIFFERENTE, different.

differenza, difference.

DIFFICILE, difficult.

DIFFICOLTÀ, difficulty.

dignità, dignity.

dimandare, to ask, to request.

DIMENTICARE, to forget.

dimentichEvole, forgetful.

dimorare, to dwell.

dimostrare, to show.

DIO (IDDIO), God.

DIRE, to say, to tell.

dirett-o(-ore),direct(-or).

direzione, direction.

DIRITTO, straight, upright, (also law, right).

disagio, hardship.

disarmare, to disarm.

disastro, disaster.

disavvantaggio, disadvantage.

DISAVVENTURA, mishap.

discolpa, excuse.

discortese, uncivil.

discosto, remote.

discreto, discreet.

disfatta, defeat.

DISGRAZIA, disaster, misfortune.

disgusto, disgust.

disleale, disloyal.

DISOCCUPATO, unoccupied.

DISONESTO, dishonest.

DISÓRDINE, disorder, confusion.

dispaccio, despatch.

DISPARIRE, disappear.

DISPIACERE, to displease, displeasure.

dispiacEvole, unpleasant.

dispregiare, to despise.

dispregio, contempt.

DISPUTA, dispute, argument.

dissimile, unlike.

dissoluto, dissolute.

DISTANTE, distant.

DISTINTO, clear.

distretto, needy.

distribuire, to distribute.

disvantaggio, disadvantage.

dito, finger, inch.

dittatore, dictator.

diverso, diverse, different, various.

divertirsi, to amuse one's self.

dividere, to divide.

divisione, division.

diviso, divided.

divoto, devout.

dolce, sweet.

dolcezza, sweetness.

dolEre, to suffer, ache.

dolore (m.), pain, grief.

domanda, question, request.

domandare, to ask.

domani (also **dimani**), to-morrow.

domattina, to-morrow morning.

donna, woman[1].

dono, gift.

doppiare, to double.

doppio, double.

dormire, to sleep.

dosso, back.

dotto, learned.

dottore, doctor.

dovEre, to owe, to be obliged to.

dubbio, doubt.

dubitare, to doubt.

duce, leader.

duomo, cathedral.

duro, hard.

E

Ebbro, drunken.

ebrietà, intoxication.

eccellente, excellent.

eccessivo, excessive.

eccetto, except.

eccezione, exception.

ecclesiAstico, priest, churchman.

ECCO, behold! here is.

edifIcio, edifice.

editore, editor, publisher.

edizione, edition.

EDUCARE, to educate.

effetto, effect.

efficace, efficacious.

eguale, equal.

egualità, equality.

ELEGANTE, elegant.

ELEMENTO, element.

eletto, chosen.

[1] **Donna** is also a title (Lady —).

109

ELETTRICO, *electric.*
elUdere, *to elude.*
emigrare, *to emigrate.*
EMPIĚRE, *to fill.*
energía, *energy.*
enErgico, *energetic.*
enorme, *enormous.*
ENTRARE, *to enter.*
ENTRATA, *entrance.*
ERA, *era.*
ERBA, *herb, grass.*
erede, *heir.*
eretto, *erect.*
erOe, *hero.*
erOico, *heroic.*
errare, *to wander.*
errore (m.), *error.*
erto, *steep.*
ESAMINARE, *to ex-amine.*
esatto, *exact.*
ESEMPIO, *example.*
ESERCITO, *army.*
ESERCIZIO, *exercise.*
esistenza, *existence.*
Esito, *issue, exit.*
ESPERIENZA, *experi-ence.*
esperimento, *experiment.*
ESPERTO, *expert.*
esplicare, *to explain.*
esposizione, *exposition, exhibition.*
espressione, *expression.*

ESPRESSO, *express.*
ESSERE, *to be.*
ESTERIORE (m), *ex-terior.*
ÉSTERO, *foreign*[1].
ESTESO, *extent.*
ESTREMO, *extreme.*
età, *age, century.*
eterno, *eternal.*
etichetta, *label, ticket.*
EVIDENTE, *evident.*
evidenza, *evidence.*
EVITARE, *to avoid.*

F
FABBRICA, *manufactory, building.*
fabbro, *smith, maker.*
facchino, *porter.*
faccia, *face.*
FACILE, *easy.*
facoltà, *faculty, power.*
FALLIRE, *to fail.*
fallo, *failure.*
FALSO, *false(ly).*
FAMA, *fame.*
FAME (fem.), *hunger.*
FAMIGLIA, *family.*
FAMOSO, *famous.*
FANCIULLO, *young boy*
fantería, *infantry.*
fardello, *bundle.*
FARE, *to do, to make.*
farina, *flour.*
farmacista, *apothecary.*

[1] **all' éstero,** *abroad.*

110

FASCIO[1] *bundle, bunch.*
FATALE, *fatal.*
faticare, *to fatigue.*
fato, *fate.*
fatto, *made (also n. fact).*
FAVORE (masc.) ,*favour.*
favorire, *to be so kind as.*
febbre (fem.), *fever.*
FEDE (f.), *faith.*
fedEle, *faithful.*
fedeltà, *fidelity.*
felicità, *felicity.*
felicitare, *to make happy; also to congratulate.*
FEMMININO, *feminine, female.*
fEria, *holiday, feast-day.*
fermo, *stopped, fixed, firm.*
feroce, *ferocious.*
ferraio, *ironmonger.*
FERRO, *iron.*
ferrovia, *railway.*
fErtile, *fertile.*
festa, *holiday, festival.*
fiamma, *flame.*
fianco, *flank, side.*
FIASCO, *bottle, flask.*
fidanza, *confidence.*

fidanzare, *to warrant, to betroth.*
fieno, *hay.*
fiero, *fierce, cruel, proud.*
fiEvole, *feeble.*
FIGLIA } *daughter.*
figliola }
FIGLIO } *son.*
figliolo }
figura, *figure.*
fila, *row.*
filo, *thread, string, wire.*
FINALE, *final.*
fine (fem.), *end.*
fine (masc.), *aim.*
finestra, *window.*
fIngere, *to feign, dissemble.*
FINIRE, *to finish.*
fino, *fine, nice, thin.*
fioco, *hoarse, dim, weak.*
FIORE (masc.), *flower.*
FIRMA, *signature.*
FIRMARE, *to sign.*
fisco, *exchequer.*
FISSO, *fixed, firm.*
fiume (m.), *river.*
flotta, *fleet.*
FLUIDO, *fluid.*

[1] From the word **FASCIO** meaning a bundle or bunch (from the **fasces** or emblem of the old Roman lictors) come many words dealing with the Italian Fascist movement, dating from the foundation in March 1919 by Sig. Benito Mussolini (Il Duce, The Leader) of the first *Fascio di Combattimento* at Milan. The word **Fascio** is used figuratively to denote the close union of adherents of the movement. There is the **Partito Nazionale Fascista**, *the National Fascist Party*, of which the members are **Fascisti**, etc., etc.

foglia, *leaf.*
foglio, *sheet of paper.*
folto, *thick, dense.*
fondamento, *foundation.*
fondare, *to found.*
fondo, *deep; also bottom* (n.)
fontana, *fountain.*
fOrbici (plur.), *scissors.*
FORCHETTA, *table fork.*
foresta, *forest.*
forestiere, *stranger.*
FORMA, *form.*
formaggio, *cheese.*
formare, *to form.*
formica, *ant.*
formosità, *beauty.*
formosa, *beautiful.*
fornaio, *baker.*
forno, *oven.*
FORTE, *strong, brave.*
FORTUNA, *fortune, good luck.*
FORZA, *force.*
FORZARE, *to force.*
fosco, *dark.*
fossa, *ditch, grave.*
fotografía, *photograph.*
fotOgrafo, *photographer.*
fracassare, *to smash.*
fracasso, *noise, hubbub.*
FRAGILE, *frail.*
fragranza, *fragrance.*
FRANCO, *free, franc.*
francobollo, *postage stamp.*

¹ also written **frodare.**

frAngere, *to break.*
FRASE (f.), *phrase, sentence.*
FRATELLO, *brother.*
fraudare¹, *to defraud.*
FREDDO, *cold.*
freno, *bit, bridle.*
fresco, *fresh, cool.*
fretta, *haste.*
frIgido, *frigid.*
frittata, *omelet.*
fritto, *fried.*
FRONTE (f.), *front.*
frutta, *fruit.*
fuga, *flight.*
fuggíre, *to flee from.*
fumare, *to smoke.*
FUMO, *smoke.*
FUOCO (foco), *fire.*
FUORI, *except ; also outside* (adv.)
furia, *fury.*
furto, *theft.*
FUTURO, *future.*

G

gaio, *gay.*
gallo, *cock.*
gana, *eagerness.*
gancio, *hook.*
garantire, *to warrant.*
gatto, *cat.*
GAS, *gas.*
gazzetta, *newspaper.*
GELARE, *to freeze.*
gelata, *frost, ice.*

112

gelato, *frozen, cold ; ice-cream,*

gElido, *frozen, very cold.*

gelo, *ice, frost.*

generale, *general.*

GENERE (m.), *kind, sort, species.*

generoso, *generous.*

gEnio, *genius.*

GENTE (f.), *people.*

gentilezza, *gentility, kindness.*

gesto, *gesture.*

gettare, *to throw, to cast.*

GIACERE, *to lie down.*

GIALLO, *yellow.*

giardino, *garden.*

GIOCARE, *to play (games), frolic, gamble.*

ginocchio, *knee.*

giocondo, *joyful.*

giocoso, *jocose.*

gioia, *jewel ; also joy.*

giornale (m.), *journal, daily.*

giornata, *day, journey, day's work.*

GIORNO, *day.*

GIOVANE, *young.*

GIOVINEZZA, *youth, youthfullness.*

gioventù (f.), *youth, young man.*

girare, *to turn.*

giro, *turn.*

GIUDICARE, *to judge.*

giUdice, *judge.*

GIUDIZIO, *judgment, prudence; court of justice.*

GIUNGERE *to arrive at.*

giunta, *arrival, meeting.*

giuOco, *game, play.*

GIURARE, *to swear.*

GIUSTIZIA, *justice.*

GIUSTO, *just, right, upright.*

GLOBO, *globe.*

GLORIA, *glory.*

glorioso, *glorious.*

GOCCIA, *drop.*

godEre, *to enjoy, rejoice.*

gola, *throat, glutton.*

GOMMA, *gum, rubber.*

gota, *cheek.*

governare, *to steer, govern.*

GOVERNO, *government.*

grAcile, *slender, delicate.*

gradEvole, *agreeable, pleasing.*

gradimento, *approval, acceptance, pleasure.*

GRADO, *degree, dignity.*

GRADUALE, *gradual.*

grammAtica, *grammar.*

GRANDE, *great.*

grandezza, *greatness.*

grano, *grain, corn, wheat.*

grasso, *fat.*

grato, *grateful.*

grave, *grave.*

grazia, *grace.*

GRAZIE ! *thanks.*

grazioso, *graceful, agreeable.*

grido, *cry.*

grosso, *big, coarse.*

GRUPPO, *group.*

GUADAGNARE, *to gain, to earn.*

guadagno, *gain.*

guanto, *glove.*

guardare, *to look.*

GUARDIA, *guard, sentry.*

guarire, *to cure.*

guarnire, *to furnish.*

guastare, *to spoil, to waste.*

guasto, *ruin, waste.*

GUERRA, *war.*

GUIDA, *guide.*

guidare, *to guide.*

GUSTARE, *to taste.*

GUSTO, *taste.*

gustoso, *pleasing.*

I

IDEA, *idea.*

idiota, *idiot.*

ignorante, *ignorant.*

IGNORARE, *not to know.*

ignoto, *unknown.*

IGNUDO (nudo), *naked, nude.*

ILLEGALE, *illegal.*

illustrare, *to illustrate.*

imbarcarsi (per), *to embark (for).*

imbrogliare, *to perplex.*

imbroglio, *perplexity, trouble, tangle.*

IMITARE, *to imitate.*

imitazione, *imitation.*

IMMAGINARE, *to imagine.*

IMMAGINAZIONE, *imagination.*

IMMATURO, *immature.*

IMMEDIATO, *immediate.*

IMMENSO, *immense.*

immondo, *filthy.*

IMMORTALE, *immortal.*

IMPARARE, *to teach, to learn.*

impedire, *to hinder.*

impegnare, *to pledge.*

imperatore[1], *emperor.*

IMPERFETTO, *imperfect.*

IMPERITO, *unskilled.*

IMPERO, *empire.*

impiegare, *to employ.*

IMPIEGATO, *employee, clerk.*

implorare, *to implore.*

IMPORTANTE, *important.*

importare, *to import ; to matter.*

IMPOSSIBILE, *impossible*

imposta, *tax.*

---

[1] Fem. **Imperatrice,** *Empress.*

impotenza, *weakness.*

IMPRESA, *enterprise.*

impressione (f.), *impression.*

ímprobo, *wicked, impossible.*

improvviso, *unexpected.*

INABILE, *incapable.*

inabilità, *inability.*

inabitAbile, *unInhabitable.*

incamminare, *to begin, to set on foot.*

INCAPACE, *incapable.*

INCERTO, *uncertain.*

inchiesta, *inquest.*

inchinarsi, *to bend, incline.*

inchiostro, *ink.*

INCHIUDERE, *to include.*

inclinare, *to incline.*

INCÓGNITO, *unknown.*

incOlto, *uncultivated.*

incominciare, *to start, to begin.*

incomodare, *to trouble.*

INCÓMODO, *inconvenient.*

incompetente, *incompetent.*

INCONTRARE, *to meet.*

incontrarsi, *to fall in with.*

incorporare, *to incorporate.*

incuria, *negligence.*

indegno, *unworthy.*

INDICARE, *to indicate.*

INDICE (m.), *index.*

indimenticAbile, *unforgettable.*

indiretto, *indirect.*

indirizzare, *to show, to direct.*

INDIRIZZO, *direction.*

indisposto, *indisposed.*

INDIVIDUO, *individual, fellow.*

indiviso, *undivided.*

indízio, *sign, indication.*

INDOLE (f.), *natural disposition, character.*

INEGUALE, *unequal.*

INFAME, *infamous.*

INFEDELE, *unfaithful.*

INFELICE, *unhappy.*

INFERIORE, *inferior.*

infermarsi, *to fall sick.*

infermo, *infirm.* (also n. *patient, sick person).*

inferno, *hell.*

Infimo, *lowest, vilest.*

INFINE, *at last.*

infinità, *infinity.*

inflnIto, *endless.*

influenza, *influence, authority, influenza.*

informare, *to inform.*

INFORMAZIONE, *information.*

informe, *shapeless.*

- **INGANNARE**, to deceive.
- **INGANNARSI**, to be mistaken.
- ingann**E**vole, deceitful.
- inganno, deceit, mistake.
- ingegn**E**re, engineer.
- **INGEGNO**, natural talent, genius.
- ingiuria, injury, wrong.
- **INGIUSTO**, unjust.
- ingordo, greedy.
- ingozzare, to swallow.
- ingrandire, to increase.
- **INGRATO**, ungrateful.
- ingresso, entrance, arrival.
- ingrosso, wholesale.
- **INIMICO**, enemy.
- **IN**I**ZIO**, beginning.
- innamorarsi, to fall in love.
- innato, inborn.
- inno, hymn.
- inquieto, restless.
- insania, madness.
- **INSEGNA**, flag, sign.
- **INSENSATO**, foolish.
- insens**í**bile, insensible.
- **INSIEME**, together.
- insetto, insect.
- insigne, notable.
- **INS**I**STERE**, to insist.
- ins**O**lito, unusual, rare.
- insulto, insult.
- intatto, untouched.
- integrale, integral.

- **í**ntegro, upright.
- intelletto, intellect.
- **INTELLIGENTE**, intelligent.
- **INTENDERE**, to understand, hear.
- **INTENSO**, intense.
- intentare, to attempt.
- intento, attentive.
- **INTERESSANTE**, interesting.
- **INTERESSE**/(m.), interest
- **INTERIORE** (m.), interior.
- interno (adj.), interior.
- investigare, to enquire.

L

- labbro (plur. -a), lip.[1]
- laborioso, laborious.
- ladro, thief, robber.
- lago, lake.
- l**A**grima, tear.
- lagrimare, to weep.
- l**A**mina, blade.
- l**A**mpada, lamp.
- lana, wool.
- **LAPIS** (masc.), pencil, crayon.
- larghezza, largeness, width.
- **LARGO**, broad, wide, bountiful.
- **LASCIARE**, to leave, abandon.

[1] **Labbro** is masculine in the singular and feminine in the plural.

LASSO, tired.

LATO, side.

LATTE (masc.), milk.

lattuga, lettuce.

LAVARE, to wash.

LAVORARE, to work, labour.

LAVORO, work.

leale, loyal.

lega, league.

legale, legal.

LEGGE (f.), law.

LEGGĔRE, to read.

LEGGERO, light.

legno, wood.

LEGUME (masc.), vegetable.

LENTO, slow.

leone, lion. (Also lione).

LETTERA, letter.

LETTO, bed.

LETTORE, reader.

levare, to raise.

LEVARSI, to get up.

LEZIONE, lesson.

LIBBRA, pound, (weight)

liberale, liberal.

liberare, to free.

LIBERO, free, frank.

libertà, liberty.

libraio, bookseller.

librería, bookseller's shop.

LIBRO, book.

lido, shore.

lieto, joyous.

lieve, light, easy.

LIMITE (masc.), limit.

limone (masc.), lemon.

limOsina, alms.

lindo, neat.

LINEA, line.

LINGUA, tongue, language.

LIQUIDO, liquid, fluid.

lira sterlina, pound sterling.

lista, list

litro, litre.

lodare, to praise.

lode (fem.), praise.

LÓGICO, logical.

LONTANO, distant.

lottare, to wrestle.

LUCE (fem.), light.

lucro, gain.

lUgubre, mournful.

LUNA, moon.

lunghezza, length.

LUNGO, long.

luogo, place.

lupo, wolf.

lusingare, to flatter.

lusso, luxury.

lustrare, to shine (trans.).

lutto, mourning.

M

macchia, stain.

MACCHINA, machine.

madonna, lady, (Virgin Mary).

MADRE, *mother.*
maestà, *majesty.*
maestro, *master.*
MAGGIORE, *bigger, greater.*
magro, *meagre, thin.*
MALATTIA, *sickness.*
malcreato, *impolite, ill-bred.*
MALE (m.), *evil, ill.*
malgrado, *in spite of.*
malizia, *malice.*
MALSANO, *unhealthy.*
mancare, *to want, to lack.*
mancia, *tip, gratuity.*
manco, *defective, want;* (adj.) *wanting.*
MANDARE, *to send.*
MANGIARE, *to eat.*
MANIERA, *manner.*
MANIFATTURA, *manufacture.*
manifesto, *manifest.*
MANO, *hand.*
mantenere, *to maintain.*
maraviglia, *wonder.*
maravigliarsi, *to wonder.*
marcare, *to mark.*
MARCO, *mark.*
MARE (masc.), *sea.*
marea, *tide.*
marina, *sea-coast.*
marinaio, *mariner.*
marino, *maritime.*

MARITO, *husband.*
marmo, *marble.*
martello, *hammer.*
maschile, *manly.*
maschio, *male, manly.*
matemAtica, *mathematics.*
matEria, *matter.*
matrimOnio, *matrimony*
MATTINA, *morning.*
matto, *mad.*
MEDESIMO, *same, self* (Fr. même).
MEDICINA, *medicine.*
MEDICO, *physician.*
MEDIO, *middle.*
MEGLIO, *better.*
mela, *apple.*
MEMORIA, *memory.*
mendicare, *to beg.*
MENTE (f.), *mind.*
MENZOGNA, *falsehood.*
MERCANTE, *merchant.*
MERCATO, *market place.*
MERITO, *merit, reward.*
meschino, *miserable, mean.*
MESE (masc.), *month.*
messaggero, *messenger.*
METODO, *method.*
METRO, *metre.*
METTERE, *to put, to set.*
MEZZO, *middle, half.*
miele (masc.), *honey.*
MILITARE, *military.*

minestra (-one), broth, soup.

ministero, administration

ministro, minister.

MINUTO, small, (also minute).

mira, aim, sight.

miserAbile, miserable.

MISERIA, misery.

MISERICORDIA, compassion, mercy.

misterioso, mysterious.

MISTURA, mixture.

MÓBILE, moveable, fickle.

MODA, mode, fashion.

MODELLO, model.

MODERATO, moderate.

MODERNO, modern.

MODESTO, modest.

MODO, manner, mood.

MOGLIE, wife, woman.

MOLLE, soft.

moltiplicare, to multiply.

moltiplicazione, multiplication.

MOLTO, very, many, much.

MOMENTO, moment.

monarca, monarch.

MONDO, world.

MONETA, coin, money.

MONTAGNA, mountain.

MONTARE, to ascend.

MONTE, (masc.) mountain.

MONUMENTO, monument.

mortalità, morality.

morbo, disease.

MORIRE, to die.

MORTE (fem.), death.

MORTO, dead.

mosca, fly.

mosso (p.p.) moved.

mostarda, mustard.

MOSTRA, sample, show.

MOSTRARE, to show.

moto, movement, motion.

movimento, movement.

multa, fine.

municipale, municipal.

MUOVĔRE (mOvere), to move, incite, to go.

muraglia, wall.

museo, museum.

MUSICA, music.

musicista, musician.

MUTO, dumb.

N

NASCERE, to be born.

NASO, nose.

NATURA, nature.

NATURALE, natural.

naufrAgio, shipwreck.

nave, (fem.) ship (large).

NAZIONE, nation.

NECESSITÀ, necessity.

NEGARE, to deny.

NEGLIGERE, to neglect.

NEGOZIARE, to negotiate.

NEMICO, ememy.

NERO, black.

netto, clean.

NEVE (fem.), snow.

nevicare, to snow.

nido, nest.

NIENTE, nothing.

nipOte, nephew, niece.

NO, no, not.

nObile, nobleman, noble.

noce (fem.), nut, walnut.

NOME (masc.), name.

nominare, to name.

NON, not, no.

NOTA, note, mark.

NOTIZIA, notice.

NOTTE (fem.), night.

novità, novelty.

NUDO, naked.

NUMERO, number.

NUOVO, new.

O

obbediente, obedient.

occhiali, spectacles.

occhio, eye.

OCEANO, ocean.

ODIO, hatred.

offEndere, to offend.

OFFERTA, offer.

officina, work-shop.

OFFRIRE, to offer.

OGGETTO, object.

OGGI, to-day.

OGNI, every, all.

OLIO, oil.

oliva (also **uliva**), olive.

onda, wave.

onestà, honesty.

ONESTO, honest.

onorario, fee, stipend, salary.

onore (masc.), honour

onta, shame.

ontoso, shameful.

ÓPERA, work, opera.

opposto, opposite.

OPPRIMERE, to oppress

ORA, hour.

orare, to pray.

orario, time table.

ordinario, ordinary.

ORECCHIO, ear.

orgOglio, pride.

ORIGINE (fem.), origin.

orizzonte(masc.),horizon.

ORO, gold.

orologio, watch, clock.

orríbile, horrible.

osare, to dare.

oscurità, obscurity.

oscuro, obscure.

ospedale(masc.), hospital.

OSSERVARE, to observe.

osservatore, observer.

osso, bone. (pl. **le ossa.**)

oste, host, innkeeper.

osteria, *inn, hostelry.*
ostíle, *hostile.*
ostinato, *obstinate.*
ÓTTIMO, *best.*
Ozio, *leisure, idleness.*

P

pacchetto, *packet.*
PACE (fem.), *peace.*
PADRE, *father.*
padrone, *master.*
PAESE (masc.), *country.*
paga, *pay.*
PAGARE, *to pay.*
PAGINA, *page* (of a book).
paglia, *straw.*
paga, *payment.*
paio, *pair.* (pl. **le paia.**)
palazzo, *palace.*
PANE (masc.), *bread.*
PANNO, *stuff* (cloth).
papa, *pope.*
papale, *papal.*
paradiso, *paradise.*
paralelo, *parallel.*
parente, *kinsman, parent.*
parentela, *relationship, kinship.*
PARERE, *to appear.*
pari, *alike, equal.*
parlamento, *parliament.*
PARLARE, *to speak.*
PAROLA, *word.*
parrOcchia, *parish.*

PARTE (fem.), *part, place.*
partenza, *departure.*
partire, *to depart.*
PARTITA, *departure ; game.*
Pasqua, *Easter.*
passAggio, *passage.*
passaporto, *passport.*
PASSARE, *to pass.*
passato, *past* (n. and adj.)
passeggiere, *passenger.*
PASSO, *step, pace.*
pasto, *food, repast.*
patata, *potato.*
PAURA, *fear.*
pausa, *pause.*
pazzo, *mad.*
peccare, *to sin.*
peccato, *sin.*
pelle (fem.), *skin.*
pelo, *hair.*
pena, *pain, punishment.*
PENNA, *feather, pen.*
PENSARE, *to think.*
pensiere (masc.), *thought.*
pentirsi, *to repent.*
PERDERE, *to lose.*
PERDONARE, *to pardon*
perdono, *pardon, forgiveness.*
PERDUTO, *lost.*
PERFETTO, *perfect.*
perfezione, *perfection.*
perícolo, *danger.*
pericoloso, *dangerous.*
perire, *to perish.*

121

perito, *expert.*
perizia, *skill.*
permanente, *permanent.*
PERMESSO, *permission.*
permEttere, *to permit.*
PERSONA, *person.*
persuadEre, *to persuade.*
PESANTE, *heavy.*
pesare, *to weigh.*
pesce, (masc.) *fish.*
PESO, *weight.*
PEZZO, *bit, piece.*
PIACERE, *to please.*
piacEvole, *pleasing.*
piAngere, *to weep.*
PIANO, *plain, level, gently, soft.*
PIANTA, *plant.*
piatto, *dish.*
PIAZZA, *place, square.*
píccolo, *small.*
PIEDE (masc.), *foot.*
piegare, *to fold.*
PIENO, *full.*
pietà, *piety, pity.*
PIETRA, *stone.*
pigro, *lazy, idle.*
pilota, *pilot.*
píngere, *to paint (also, to push).*
pío, *pious.*
PIOGGIA, *rain.*
PIOVERE, *to rain.*
pipa, *tobacco-pipe.*
pittore, *painter.*
pittura, *painting.*

piuttosto, *rather, somewhat.*
pochezza, *littleness.*
POCO, *little, few.*
PODERE, *power.*
podestà, *magistrate.*
poema (masc.), *poem.*
poesia, *poetry.*
poeta, *poet.*
poggio, *hill, hillock.*
POLITICO, *political.*
polito, *polished.*
pOllice (masc.), *thumb.*
POLLO, *chicken.*
polmone (masc.), *lungs.*
PÓLVERE (fem.), *dust, powder.*
polveroso, *dusty.*
pomo, *apple.*
ponte (masc.), *bridge.*
popolare, *popular.*
PÓPOLO, *people.*
popoloso, *populous.*
porco, *pig.*
porre, *to put.*
PORTA, *door, gate.*
PORTARE, *to carry, to wear.*
porto, *port.*
POSIZIONE, *position.*
POSSEDERE, *to possess.*
POSSIBILE, *possible.*
possibilità, *possibility.*
posta, *post.*
POTERE, *to be able.*
POVERO, *poor.*

povertà, poverty.
pranzare, to dine.
PRANZO, dinner.
PRATICA, practice.
praticare, to practice.
precauzione, precaution.
preciso, precise.
preferenza, preference.
prEmere, to press.
PRENDERE, to take, to seize.
PREPARARE, to prepare.
presa, capture, catch.
PRESENTE (n. and adj.) present (time).
preservare, to preserve.
PRESSO, near, at.[1]
PRESTARE, to lend.
PRESTO, quick.
pretEndere, to pretend.
pretesto, pretext.
prezioso, precious.
PREZZO, price.
prigione (fem.), prison.
PRIMA, before, first.
primo, first.
PRINCIPALE, principal, chief.
príncipe, prince.
principiare, to begin.
princípio, beginning.
PROBABILE, probable.
probo, upright.
professore, professor.
profondo, depth, deep.
progetto, project.

programma (masc.), programme.
PROGRESSO, progress.
PROMESSA, promise.
PRONTO, ready, at hand.
PRONUNCIARE, to pronounce.
propOsito, intention.
proprietà, property.
PROPRIO, own, proper, peculiar to.
prosa, prose.
prosciutto, ham.
PROVA, proof.
PROVARE, to try, to prove.
PROVINCIA, province.
prudente, prudent.
pulire, to clean, to polish.
PULITO, clean, polished.
PUNIRE, to punish.
PUNTO, point.
PURE, yet, even, still.
PURO, pure.

Q

qua,
QUI, } here, hither.

quadro, square, picture, painting.
QUALITÀ, quality.
QUANTITÀ, quantity.
QUESTIONE, question.
quieto, quiet, still.
quotidiano, daily.

[1] **Presso** is also used for c/o in addressing letters.

123

R

rAbbia, *fury.*

rabbioso, *enraged, furious.*

RACCOLTA, *collection, crop, harvest.*

raccomodare, *to mend.*

raccontare, *to relate.*

racconto, *account, story.*

radíce (f.), *root.*

RAGAZZO, -A, *boy-girl.*

RAGIONE (f.), *reason.*

ragno, *spider.*

ramo, *branch.*

rango, *rank.*

RAPIDO, *rapid, quick.*

rapporto, *report.*

rarità, *rarity, scarcity.*

RARO, *rare, thin, scarce.*

rata, *rate, instalment.*

razza, *race.*

RE, *king.*

reale, *royal, real, true.*

recente, *recent.*

reclamare, *to protest.*

refrigerare, *to cool.*

regalare, *to make a present of.*

regalo, *gift, present.*

rEggere, *to rule.*

regina, *queen.*

REGIONE (f.), *region.*

registrare, *to register.*

registro, *register.*

REGNO, *kingdom, reign.*

regolare, *to regulate.*

RELIGIONE, *religion.*

reo, *guilty.*

repente, *sudden(ly).*[1]

REPUBBLICA, *republic.*

resíduo, *remainder.*

respirare, *to breathe.*

respiro, *breath.*

RESTO, *remainder.*

rete (fem.), *net, network.*

retro, *backward.*

retto, *right, upright.*

ricchezza, *riches.*

RICCO, *rich.*

ricEvere, *to receive.*

ricevuta, *receipt.*

RICORDARE, *to remember, to mention.*

ricordo, *remembrance.*

ricusare, *to refuse*

RIDERE, *to laugh.*

rifiuto, *refusal.*

RIFUGIO, *refuge.*

RIGIDO, *rigid.*

rigore (m.), *rigour.*

riguardo, *look, regard.*

rilassato, *slack, relaxed.*

rima, *rhyme.*

rimanEre, *to remain.*

rimedio, *remedy.*

rimorso, *remorse.*

ringraziare, *to thank.*

rinnovare, *to renovate.*

---

[1] More common in the phrase **di repente,** suddenly.

rinomanza, *renown.*
rípido, *steep.*
ripieno, *full.*
riputazione, *reputation.*
RISA (plural), *laughter.*
risanare, *to cure.*
ríschio, *risk, danger.*
riso, *rice.*
risOlvere, *to dissolve, to resolve.*
rispetto, *respect, regard.*
RISPÓNDERE, *to answer.*
RISPOSTA, *answer.*
ristorante (m.), *restaurant.*
ristretto, *restricted.*
ritornare, *to return.*
ritto, *right, straight, just.*
riuscire, *to succeed.*
RIUSCITA, *success.*
riva, *shore, bank.*
riverso, *reverse, overflow.*
riviera, *sea-shore, river.*
rivista, *review.*
ROBA, *goods, gown.*
rOccia, *rock, precipice.*
RÓMPERE, *to break.*
rosa, *rose.*
rosso, *red.*
rostro, *beak.*
ROTONDO, *round.*
ROTTO, *broken, smashed.*
rovinare, *to ruin.*

S

sala, *hall.*
SALE (masc.), *salt.*
salsa, *sauce.*
SALUTE (fem.), *health, safety.*
SALVARE, *to save.*
salvo, *safe, except.*
sanare, *to heal.*
sAngue (masc.), *blood.*
sanità, *health.*
SANO, *sound, healthy.*
santo, *saint, holy.*
SAPERE, *to know, understand.*
sapienza, *wisdom.*
SAPONE (masc.), *soap.*
sapore (masc.), *savour, taste.*
sarto, *tailor.*
sAvio, *wise man, (wise, adj.).*
sbadato, *negligent.*
SBAGLIAR(SI), *to be mistaken.*
SBAGLIO, *mistake, error.*
sballare, *to unpack.*
sbarcare, *to disembark.*
scafo[1], *the hull of a ship.*
scala, *stairs.*
scappare, *to escape.*
scappata, *escape, flight.*
scarlatto, *scarlet.*

[1] PirOscafo, *liner;* motoscafo, *motor-ship etc.*

scarpa, shoe.
scarso, scarce, niggardly.
SCATOLA, box, case.
scEgliere, to choose, select.
SCELTO, chosen.
scemo, deficient, silly.
scena, scene, stage.
SCENDERE, to descend.
scErněre, to discern.
scesa, descent, velocity.
schema (masc.), scheme.
schermo, defence (also screen).
scherzare, to jest, joke.
scherzo, jest.
schiavitù, slavery.
schiavo, slave.
sciente, learned, knowing, aware.
scientífico, scientific.
SCIENZA, science.
scintilla, spark, sparkle.
scioperato, idle.
scolaro, scholar.
SCÓMODO, inconvenient.
SCOPERTA, discovery.
scorso, oversight.
scrittoio, writing-desk.
scrittore, writer.
scrittura, writing, scripture.
SCRIVERE, to write.
SCUOLA, school.

scuro, dark, obscure.
scusare, to excuse.
SECCO, dry.
secolare, secular.
SECOLO, century, age.
SECONDO, second.
sedEre, to sit down.
sEdia, chair, seat.
sedizione, sedition.
SEGNALE(masc.),signal.
segnare, to mark.
SEGNO, sign.
segretario, secretary.
SEGRETO, secret.
seguente, following.
SEGUIRE, to follow.
selva, forest.
selvaggio, wild.
sembianza, face, appearance.
sembrare, to seem.
seme (m.), seed.
sEmplice, simple, pure.
senso, sense, meaning.
sentimento, feeling.
SENTIRE, to feel.
SEPARARE, to separate.
SERA[1], evening.
sErie (fem.), series.
serio, serious, grave.
serrare, to shut, lock.
servire, to serve.
seta, silk.
SETE (fem.), thirst.
SETTIMANA, week.

[1] Buona sera! Good evening!

severo, *severe.*
SEZIONE, *section.*
sfera, *sphere.*
sfortunato, *unhappy.*
sforzare, *to contrain.*
sforzo, *effort.*
sgarbato, *impolite.*
sghembo, *crooked, oblique*
sgradire, *to displease.*
sgraziato, *unfortunate.*
sguardo, *look, glance.*
sicurezza, *security.*
SICURO, *safe, sure.*
SIGNORA, *lady.*
SIGNORE, *gentleman.*
SIGNORIA, *lordship,*
  (*dominion*).
SIGNORINA, *young*
  lady, miss.
silenzio, *silence.*
simpAtico, *attractive,*
  charming.
sincero, *sincere.*
sinistra, *left* (hand).
SINISTRO, *left.* (also,
  accident.)
SISTEMA (masc.), *system.*
sito, *site.*
smarrire, *lose, wander.*
smontare, *to descend.*
snello, *nimble.*
soave, *sweet.*
sobrio, *sober.*
soccorso, *succour, help.*
SOCIETÀ, *society.*

SODDISFARE, *to satisfy.*
soffrire, *to suffer.*
SOGNO, *dream.*
SOLDATO, *soldier.*
sole (masc.), *sun.*
solenne, *solemn.*
SOLERE, *to be accustomed, wont.*
SÓLIDO, *solid.*
SÓLITO, *accustomed.*
SOLO, *only, alone.*
SOLTANTO, *solely.*
soma, *burden, load.*
SOMMA, *sum.*
SONARE, *to sound.*
SONNO, *sleep.*
sordo, *deaf.*
SORELLA, *sister.*
sorpresa, *surprise.*
SORTE (fem.), *fate, state,
  condition.*
sospettare, *to suspect.*
sostanza, *substance.*
sostenEre, *to support.*
sottomEttere, *to submit.*
spaventare, *to frighten.*
spavento, *fright.*
SPAZIO, *space.*
specchio, *looking-glass.*
SPECIALE, *special.*
spEcie (fem.), *species.*
spedale (masc.), *hospital.*
spedire, *to despatch.*
spedito, *prompt.*
spEndere, *to spend.*
SPERANZA, *hope.*

SPERARE, to hope.

sperienza, experience.

spesso, thick, dense.

spettAcolo, spectacle, show, display.

spiacere (intr.), to be displeased, sorry.

SPIRITO, spirit, mind.

splEndere, to shine.

SPLENDIDO, splendid.

sporcare, to soil.

SPORCO, filthy, dirty.

sposare, to marry.

stAbile, stable.

stabilire, to establish.

stabilità, stability.

STAGIONE (fem.), season, stage.

stamattina, this morning.

STAMPA, press, printing.

STAMPARE, to stamp, to print.

stamperia, printing-office

stancare, to tire.

STANCARSI, to get tired.

STANCO, tired.

STANZA, room, apartment; dwelling.

STARE, to stand, to stop, to be, to dwell.

STASERA, this evening.

STATO, state, rank.

STAZIONE, station.

stella, star.

STESSO, same.

stima, esteem.

stoffa, stuff.

stOmaco, stomach.

STÓRIA, history, story.

STRADA, road, route, way, street.

STRANIERO, foreigner.

strano, strange, shocking.

straordinario, extraordinary.

stretto, strict, narrow.

studente, student

STUDIARE, to study.

studio, study.

stupendo, surprising.

STUPIDO, stupid.

sturbare, to disturb.

SUBITO, sudden, immediately.

succEdere, to succeed, to happen.

successo, success, conclusion.

SONARE, to sound, ring, (also, to play music).

superbo, proud.

SUPERIORE, superior, better.

supErfluo, superfluous.

suppa, soup (or **zuppa**).

suppOrre, to suppose.

SUPREMO, supreme.

sussurro, murmur.

svanire, to vanish.

svantaggio, disadvantage.

svegliare, to awake.

128

.svelto, *nimble, quick.*
sventura, *misfortune.*
SVENTURATO, *unfortunate.*

T
tabacco, *tobacco.*
TACERE, *to be silent.*
tAcito, *silent.*
taciturno, *taciturn.*
TAGLIARE, *to cut, shorten.*
talento, *inclination, talent.*
tapino, *wretched, miserable.*
TARDARE, *to delay.*
TASCA, *pocket.*
tassa, *tax.*
TAVOLA, *table.*
TAZZA, *cup.*
te (masc.). *tea.*
teatro, *theatre.*
tela, *cloth, linen, painting.*
TELEFONO, *telephone.*
telEgrafo, *telegraph.*
TELEGRAMMA (masc.), *telegram.*
tema, *fear.*
TEMERE, *to fear.*
tempesta, *tempest.*
temperatura, *temperature.*
tempio, *temple.*
TEMPO, *time, weather.*
tEnebre (pl.), *darkness.*
TENERE, *to hold.*

TENTARE, *to try, attempt.*
teoría, *theory.*
TERMINARE, *to finish.*
TERRA, *earth, land.*
terreno, *land, ground.*
terríbile, *terrible.*
terrore (masc.), *terror.*
tesoro, *treasure.*
TESTA, *head.*
tetro, *dark, gloomy.*
TETTO, *roof.*
tímido, *timid.*
TIMORE (masc.), *fear.*
tirare, *to draw, shoot.*
TOCCARE, *to touch.*
tomo, *volume, book.*
tonare, *to thunder.*
toro, *bull.*
tornare, *to return, become again.*
torre (fem.), *tower.*
torrente, (masc.) *torrent.*
tosse (fem.), *cough.*
tosto, *quick, soon.*
traduzione, *translation.*
TRAFFICO, *traffic.*
tragEdia, *tragedy.*
trasmEttere, *to transmit.*
transparente, *transparent*
TRASPORTO, *transport.*
traversare, *to traverse, go across.*
TRENO, *train.*
tribunale, (masc.) *court of law.*

129

tristezza, *sadness.*
TRISTE, *sad.*
TRISTO, *bad, wicked.*
TROVARE, *to find.*
truffare, *to cheat.*
tuOno, *thunder.*

U

UBBIDIRE, *to obey.*
ubbriaco, *drunk.*
uccello, *bird.*
uccIdere, *to kill, murder.*
udienza, *audience.*
udire, *to hear.*
ufficiale, *official.*
UGUALE, *equal.*
ULTIMO, *last.*
umano, *human, humane.*
UMIDO, *moist.*
Umile, *humble.*
umiliare, *to humble.*
umiltà, *humbleness.*
uniforme, *uniform.*
UNIRE, *to unite.*
università, *university.*
UOMO, *man.* (pl. **uOmini.**)
UOVO, *egg.* (Pl. **uova**).
urgente, *urgent.*
usare, *to use.*
USCIRE, *to go out.*
USCITA, *issue, door, exit, escape.*
uso, *use.*
UTILE, *useful.*
uva, *grape.*

V

vacca, *cow.*
VAGONE (m.), *wagon.*
VALERE, *to be worth.*
vAlido, *valid, legal.*
VALIGIA, *portmanteau, valise.*
valle (fem.), *valley.*
valore (masc.), *value.*
vano, *vain.*
vantaggio, *advantage.*
vapore (masc.), *vapour, steamship.*
VARIO, *various.*
vaso, *vase, vessel.*
vasto, *immense.*
VECCHIO, *old.*
vece[1], *instead.*
VEDERE, *to see.*
vEdovo (-a), *widower widow.*
vela, *sail.*
veleno, *poison.*
VELOCE, *swift.*
vena, *vein.*
VENDERE, *to sell.*
vendetta, *vengeance.*
vendicare, *to revenge.*
VENIRE, *to come.*
VENTO, *wind.*
ventura, *fortune.*
venturo[2], *future, coming.*
venturoso, *lucky.*
verace, *true.*
VERBO, *verb, word.*

[1] In vece di, *instead of.*
[2] For example: **Il mese venturo,** *next month.*

- **VERDE**, green.
- **VERGOGNA**, shame.
- verificare, to verify.
- **VERITÀ**, truth.
- **VERO**, true.
- verso, verse.
- vestimento, dress.
- vestire, to dress.
- vezzoso, nice, charming, graceful.
- **VIA**, way, road, street.
- **VIAGGIARE**, to travel.
- **VIAGGIO**, journey.
- vicino, neighbour.
- vico, narrow lane, street
- **VIETARE**, to prohibit.
- **VIETATO**, forbidden.
- vigilare, to watch
- vigore (masc.), vigour.
- villaggio, village.
- viltà, cowardice.
- **VINCÈRE**, to conquer, defeat.
- vino, wine.
- violento, violent.
- virtù (f.), virtue.
- virtuoso, virtuous.
- visita, visit.
- **VISITARE**, to visit.
- **VISTA**, sight, view.
- vita, life; waist.
- vite, vine.
- vittoria, victory.

- vivace, sprightly.
- **VIVERE**, to live.
- **VIVO** alive
- vizio, vice.
- **VOCE** (fem.), voice.
- **VOGLIA**, will, wish.
- volare, to fly.
- **VOLENTIERI**, willingly.
- **VOLERE**, to will, to wish.
- volgo, common people, mass.
- volo, flight.
- volontà, will, wish, will-power.
- volontario, voluntary, volunteer.
- volpe (f.), fox.
- **VOLTA**[1], turn, time.
- **VOLTARE**, to turn.
- volume (masc.), volume.
- vorace, voracious.
- votare, to empty, to give one's vote, to vow.
- voto, vow, vote.

Z

- zelo, zeal.
- **ZERO**, zero.
- **ZIO**, uncle.
- zolfanello, match.
- zolfo, sulphur.
- zoppo, lame.
- **ZUCCHERO**, sugar.

[1] È la mia volta, It is my turn. Una volta, due volte, once twice, etc.

**EXTRACT TO ILLUSTRATE THE USE
AND SCOPE OF THE GRAMMAR
AND VOCABULARY IN THIS BOOK**

K

§1. FROM " THE PRINCE "
BY NICCOLÒ MACHIAVELLI.

IN CHE MODO I PRINCIPI DEBBANO OSSERVARE LA FEDE
IN WHAT WAY PRINCES MUST KEEP FAITH

Quanto sia laudabile in un principe mantenere la fede, vivere

How laudable it is in a prince to keep (good) faith, to live

con integrità e non con astuzia, ciascuno lo intende. Nondimanco si

with / by integrity and not by cunning, everyone understands. Yet, it is

vede per esperienza ne' nostri tempi, quelli principi aver fatto gran

seen by experience in our times, (that) those princes have done great

cose, che della fede hanno tenuto poco conto, e che hanno saputo con

things, who for good faith have had little regard, and who have known (how)

l'astuzia aggirare i cervelli degli uomini, ed alla fine hanno superato

by trickery to cheat men's brains, and in the end have overcome

quelli che si sono fondati en su la lealtà.

those who have founded themselves on loyalty.

Dovete adunque sapere como sono due generazioni di combattere:

You must know then that there are two ways of fighting:

l'una con le leggi, l'altra con la forza; quel primo (modo) è proprio

one with (the aid of) laws, the other with force; the first way is (an)

dell'uomo, quel secondo delle bestie; ma perchè il primo spesse volte

attribute of man, the second of beast; but because the first very often

non basta, conviene ricorrere al secondo. Pertanto, ad un principe è

is not adequate, it is expedient to (have) recourse to the second. Therefore for

necessario saper bene usare la bestia e l'uomo....

a prince it is necessary to use (the qualities of) the beast and man. . . .

Essendo adunque un principe necessitato sapere bene usare la

Being then a prince obliged to know well (how) to act as the

bestia, debbe di quella pigliare la volpe e il lione; perchè il lione

beast, he must (in that sense) equal the fox and the lion; because the lion

non si difende da' lacci, la volpe non si difende da' lupi. Bisogna

does not defend himself from snares, (nor) the fox from wolves. He must

adunque essere volpe a conoscere i lacci, e lione a sbigottire i lupi.

therefore be a fox to know snares, and a lion to frighten wolves.

135

**Coloro che stanno semplicemente in sul lione,
non se ne intendono. Non**

Those who rely simply on (qualities of) the lion, do
not understand this. For

**può pertanto un signore prudente, nè debbe,
osservare la fede, quando tale**

this reason a wise overlord cannot and ought not to
keep faith when

**osservanzia gli torni contro, e che sono spente le
cagioni che la**

such observance might turn against his interests, and
when the causes are

fecero promettere.

gone which made him pledge it.

**E se gli uomini fussero tutti buoni, questo
precetto non sarebbe**

And if men were all good, this precept would not be

buono; ma perchè sono tristi, e non la osserverebbero a te, tu ancora non

good; but because they are contemptible and will not
keep (faith) with you

**l'hai da osservare a loro. Nè mai ad un principe
mancheranno cagioni**

you have not to keep it with them. Nor to a prince
will there ever lack

**legittime di colorare la inosservanzia. Di questo
se ne potrebbe.**

legitimate reasons to colour the non-observance. Of
this it is possible

**dare infiniti esempi moderni, e mostrare quanti
paci, quante promesse**

to give infinite modern examples, and to show how
many peaces, how many

sono state fatte irrite e vane per la infedeltà dei principi; e quello
promises have been made null and void by the faith-
lessness of princes; and

che ha saputo meglio usare la volpe, è meglio capitato. Ma è necessario
that he who has known best to use (the wile of) the
fox, has best succeeded.

questa natura saperla bene colorire, ed essere gran simulatore e
But it is necessary to know well how to camouflage this
character, and to be

dissimulatore, e sono tanto semplici gli uomini, e tanto ubbidiscono alle
a great hypocrite and dissembler, and men are so
ingenuous, and so greatly

necessità presenti, che colui che inganna troverà sempre chi si lascerà
obey present necessities, that he who deceives will
find always one who

ingannare. . . .
allows himself to be duped. . . .

Ad un principe adunque non è necessario avere in fatto tutte le
For a prince then it is not necessary in fact to have
all the

soprascritte qualità, ma è ben necessario parer di averle. Anzi ardirò
above-mentioned qualities, but it is very necessary to
seem to have them. Indeed

di dire questo, che avendole ed osservandole sempre, sono dannose; e
I will go (so far as) to say this, that to have them and
act on them always

parendo d'averle, sono utili : come parer pietoso, fidele, umano, religioso,

is harmful, while to appear to have them is beneficial: also to seem compassionate,

intero, ed essere; ma stare in modo edificato con l'animo che bisognando

faithful, humane, religious, reliable and to be so; but to be so (constituted) in mind, that not needing to

non essere, tu possa e sappia mutare il contrario. Ed hassi ad intendere

be (and of these), you can and know (how) to change to the opposite. And you must

questo, che un principe, e massime un principe nuovo, non può osservare tutte

grasp this, that a prince, and above all a new prince, cannnot observe all

quelle cose per le quali gli uomini sono tenuti buoni, essendo spesso

those things by which men are esteemed good, being often

necessitato per mantenere lo stato operare contro alla fede, contro alla

driven in order to maintain the state to act contrary to good faith, against

carità, contro alla umanità, contro alla religione. E però bisogna che

charity, against humanity against religion. And therefore it behoves him

egli abbia un animo disposto a volgersi secondo che i venti e le

to have }
that he have } a mind disposed to turn according as the winds and the

variazioni della fortuna gli comandano; e come di sopra dissi, non partirsi

fluctuations of fortune command it ; and as I have said above, not to go away

dal bene potendo, ma sapere entrare nel mal necessitato. . . .

from what is good if possible, but to know how to enter into unavoidable evil. . . .

Faccia adunque un principe conto di vincere e mantenere lo

Let a prince then take care to overcome difficulties and maintain

stato, i mezzi saranno sempre giudicati onorevoli, e da ciascuno lodati;

the state, (and) the means will always be judged honourable, and praised by everyone;

perchè il vulgo ne va sempre preso con quello che pare e con

because the rabble are always taken in by appearances and result

l'evento della cosa, e nel mondo non è se non vulgo; e i pochi ci hanno

of a thing, and in the world there is only rabble; and the few find

luogo, quando gli assai non hanno dove appoggiarsi.

place there, while the many have not anywhere to lean against.

Alcuno principe dei presenti tempi, quale non è bene nominare, e,

A certain prince of the present times, whom it is not well to name,

non predica mai altro che pace e fede; e dell'una e dell'altra è

never preaches anything but peace and good faith; and of both he is

inimicissimo; a l'una e l'altra, quando e' l'avesse osservata, gli arrebbe

the greatest enemy; and had he observed either the one or the other, he

più volte tolto o la riputazione o lo stato[1].

would many times have lost both reputation and state.

[1] The example given above is based on the Italian critical text of Mario Casella. The spelling is, however, modernised. In a few instances Machiavelli's words and phrases have become archaic, but otherwise the student who has worked through this book should be able to follow the meaning.

* * *

STATISTICAL NOTE

Total essential words in Vocabulary in Part II	=	1650
Structural and other words in Part I	=	350
Total (approximately)	=	2000

Of these about 800 general and 250 structural words are given in large type: a total of 1150. The large type words in this book may be considered as a first approximation to a ' Basic Vocabulary ' of the Italian language.

THE END

BASIC ENGLISH

Basic English is a system in which 850 English words do all the work of over 20,000 and so give to everyone a second or international language which will take as little of the learner's time as possible.

THE SYSTEM

Basic English.
A general account, with Word-list and Rules.

The Basic Words.
A full account of the 850, with senses in French and German.

The A B C of Basic English[1]
A simple account, step by step, for learners and teachers.

Basic Step by Step[2]
The words in 30 groups, for teaching, with Notes and Pictures.

The Basic Dictionary
Putting into Basic the 7,500 words most used in Normal English.

Basic for Business
A complete system for international trade, with examples of letters.

Basic for Science
How Basic takes science to the International level ; with examples covering the chief branches.

Basic for Economics
Covering the theory, with examples from representative writers.

Basic for Geology
Examples from this special field of what Basic is able to do with material for experts.

The Sounds and Forms of Basic English
Suggestions for talking with a natural rhythm.

EXAMPLES

Basic by Examples.   Every Basic word with its different uses.
Everyday Basic.   Simple examples for all purposes.
Brighter Basic.   For young persons of taste and feeling.
Keäwe's Bottle.   Stevensons' " The Bottle Imp " in Basic.
Pinocchio.   Collodi's story in a short Basic form.
Gulliver in Lilliput.   The first of Gulliver's journeys.
Robinson Crusoe.   His story in Basic.
Wise Words of an Early American.   Benjamin Franklin.
Stories from France.   From the prose of Perrault.
Stories from China.   A selection by T. K. Ch'u.
The Two Friends.   Tourgenieff's moving story.
Stories for the Young.   And for the not so young. By Tolstoi.

[1] And in French, German, Spanish, Italian and Dutch. (Price 3/6).
[2] And in French, German, Spanish, Italian and Dutch. (Price 3/6).

The Gold Insect. Poe's " Gold Bug " put into Basic.
Julius Caesar. From North's Plutarch (with " Brutus ").
Japanese Stories. From Lafcadio Hearn.
The Three Signs. Stories by Hawthorne, Irving, and Poe.
That Night. Tumura's " Sono Yo " in Basic.
The Organization of Peace. By Maxwell Garnett.
International Talks. By Wickham Steed, with Basic parallel.
From Pictures to Letters. For the youngest. By Ellen Walpole.
Basic by Isotype. With Dr. Neurath's pictures.
Lamb's Stories from Shakespeare. A Basic selection.
Stories from Hans Andersen. Basic by C. Hughes Hartmann.
Stories from the Bible. A selection from the Basic Bible.
The Basic St. Mark. The first complete unit.
The Basic St. John. Basic by the Rev. Edwin Smith.
The Song of Songs. Basic by Ma Than É. With Ecclesiastes.
The Meno of Plato. Basic by J. Rantz.
The Chemical History of a Candle. Faraday in Basic.
Science and Well-Being. A selection from J. B. S. Haldane.
The Outlook of Science. A further selection from Prof. Haldane.
A Basic Astronomy. By S. L. Salzedo.
The Story of Letters and Numbers. By C. L. T. Griffith.
Black Beauty. Anna Sewell's story. For school use.
Death in High Society. Strange stories by Inez Holden.
Carl and Anna. Leonhard Frank's story. Not for school use.

GENERAL

Basic English versus the Artificial Languages.
The arguments against Esperanto, Ido and the rest. By C. K. Ogden.
Basic in Teaching : East and West
The value of Basic in education. By Dr. I. A. Richards.
Basic Rules of Reason (In Basic)
Basic as an Instrument of thought. By Dr. I. A. Richards.
Statement and Suggestion. (In Basic)
Basic as an instrument for reading verse. By A. P. Rossiter.
International Picture Language. (In Basic)
The signs and pictures now international. By Dr. Otto Neurath.
Word Economy
Word-selection in relation to expansions and fictions.

By L. W. Lockhart.

All 3/6 a copy

Records. By J. C. Catford (2, double-sided), 10/- (plus 2/6 purchase tax).

Panopticon. 3/6.

THE ORTHOLOGICAL INSTITUTE
45, GORDON SQUARE, LONDON, W.C.1